PLANNI
USE CLAS

A Guide to the
Use Classes Orders

PLANNING USE CLASSES

A Guide to the

Use Classes Orders

Second Edition

ROBERT HOME
MA, PhD, DipTP, MRTPI
Town Planning Consultant

BSP PROFESSIONAL BOOKS

OXFORD LONDON EDINBURGH

BOSTON MELBOURNE

First Edition published 1987
Second Edition published 1989

British Library
Cataloguing in Publication Data

Home, Robert
  Planning use classes. — 2nd ed
  1. Great Britain. Commercial property.
  Development. Control. Law
  I. Title
  344.1064'4

ISBN 0-632-02586-7

BSP Professional Books
Editorial Offices:
Osney Mead, Oxford OX2 0EL
  (Orders: Tel. 0865 240201)
8 John Street, London WC1N 2ES
23 Ainslie Place, Edinburgh EH3 6AJ
3 Cambridge Center,
  Suite 208, Cambridge
  MA 02142, USA
107 Barry Street, Carlton
  Victoria 3053, Australia

Set Burns & Smith, Derby
Printed and bound in Great Britain by
Mackays of Chatham PLC, Chatham,
Kent

Contents

Introduction
to First Edition

It was only a few days before the announcement of the date for the 1987 General Election when the Secretary of State for the Environment Nicholas Ridley, in a written answer in the House of Commons announced an apparently obscure but eagerly-awaited statutory instrument, aimed to benefit business users of property — the Town and Country Planning (Use Classes) Order 1987 (UCO). Politically the timing was good because, while a technical document not readily understood, the reform of the UCO had already aroused unexpected controversy. As it happened, the political parties were soon embroiled in General Election campaigning and the minutiae of planning regulations were overshadowed by wider issues, so the new Order came into effect unnoticed except by those professionally involved with planning and property development.

As befits the seriousness of the issues with which it deals, the new Order was a long time in preparation. It was not issued until nearly two years after the Government first announced its 'fundamental review' of the UCO in a White Paper on deregulation. The reforms had proved more complex and contentious than at first anticipated, not least because the report of the Property Advisory Group, the first stage in the reform process, contained some radical proposals. The Government bowed to pressure from residents' groups to drop ideas for releasing more home-based business activity from planning control. Another unpopular proposal, to create one large shops class to include retailing, services and prepared food, proved too radical for property developers and managers who feared the consequences for the mix of uses in, and hence the attractiveness of, shopping centres.

Even without some of the more radical reform proposals, the 1987 Order is very important for town planning and the property industry, removing many changes of use from planning control. While only a statutory instrument and needing little modification to primary legislation, it represents the biggest change to the planning system since the public participation and conservation measures of the early 1970s. The UCO has been one of the key components of the planning system introduced in 1947, and the 1987 Order is the most drastic revision of the UCO since then. Compared with it, the three previous changes (1950, 1963 and 1972, not counting minor amendments) were mere tinkerings.

The main reform in the new Order is undoubtedly the new business class, which merges light industry, offices, and studio/laboratory uses into one class. This aroused as much opposition as other proposals that were abandoned, but the Government stood firm by the commitment, which it saw as essential to ease bureaucratic restraints upon business. Its justification was largely based upon the flexibility which the new class gave for new 'high-tech' development, but the consequences of the new class may be greater for the thousands of existing light industrial premises, especially in inner city areas. There will now be a greater freedom to convert industrial floorspace to studio workshops or offices, bypassing council planning policies aimed at protecting blue-collar employment opportunities. The distinctive character of areas like Soho and Covent Garden may be eroded as service industries are displaced by higher-value office uses — as the Savoy Tailors recognized when they lobbied in Parliament to stop the new class.

Although the business class may be the main reform, and has certainly attracted the most attention, the 1987 Order has altered every use class (except the special industrial classes) with implications for practically every area of planning control. Two new classes have been introduced — the food and drink class and the dwellinghouses class — and others merged or enlarged in their scope. Among the changes with major effects are the re-incorporation of hostels in the hotels class, and a more widely-drawn assembly and leisure class, which may change the face of much of our countryside and coastal areas.

As well as redrawing the use classes, the 1987 Order also clarifies some areas of uncertainty in planning control, usually with the effect of reducing the scope of control. Subdivision of planning units (other than dwellinghouses) is, since the Housing and Planning Act 1986, not development and therefore outside planning control. Use class rights now clearly apply to land whether or not it is associated with a building. Intensification within a use class is now almost impossible to establish for enforcement purposes. One innovation has been to specify certain uses which are excluded from any use class and are therefore *sui generis*.

While some areas of uncertainty have been clarified, one can expect important new case law to be made as fresh matters of legal interpretation are challenged on appeal. The UCO has been given a new look — the confusing Roman numerals of previous Orders are replaced with letters and titles for easy reference, and sometimes confusing definitions are tidied up — but also new terms and concepts are introduced which are sometimes not defined. Offices, formerly in one class, have now been split between two mutually exclusive classes, and new tests of levels of public access and environmental acceptability will have to be applied. Among the undefined terms are 'storage and distribution' (which replace the old warehousing class) and 'assembly and leisure', and even with the wider use class boundaries there is still room for dispute over how the boundaries should be drawn (for instance between the hotels and residential institutions classes).

Interpretation and implementation problems are to be expected under any new regulatory regime, but with the 1987 Order some of these problems may be made worse by the narrow perspective of the reforms. Not only did the working group which produced the proposals not include a local government planner, but its attitude to local planning authorities was generally one of suspicion, and its understanding of the objectives of planning control limited. The disapproving attitude struck towards conditions restricting use class rights is but one example of this attitude. Some critics of the proposals felt that they would benefit those in the property business as developers and landlords, but would not necessarily benefit business tenants and certainly not residents, and would be unlikely to improve amenity and the environment. Planning aims like protecting the character of an area, setting environmental standards for new development, and managing traffic seem to have weighed little with the working group or the Government. While much of the UCO may indeed be out of date and an unnecessary constraint on business, environmental safeguards have generally evolved because the public support them, and these controls can themselves help to create new business and employment, not only in the public sector but in building design and materials and the manufacture of environmental control and monitoring equipment.

As stated in circular 13/87 (which accompanied the 1987 Order), the approach of the Order is not to require planning permission for types of development 'that generally do not damage amenity', while keeping control over changes of use 'that would have a material impact, in land-use planning terms, on the local amenity or environment'. Amenity and environmental effects are notoriously subjective and difficult to assess, but one can anticipate surprise and concern when residents find that their local council is powerless to act against a new and unwelcome use of land because the 1987 Order has effectively removed it from planning control, e.g. a leisure use in a Green Belt area, an intensification of small business activity in a residential area, or a café becoming a public house or a wine bar.

As well as the local political consequences from disgruntled residents, tenants and users of commercial property may be adversely affected. High quality office parks may find industrial activities creeping in, resulting in more loading and unloading of goods vehicles, conflicts over road and parking space, and more noise. Where a business park is tightly controlled through lease restrictions by a single landlord such problems are unlikely, but this is not the situation in many areas, especially where premises are owner-occupied. Perhaps the opposite trend is more likely, with industrial tenants being displaced by office uses.

The new Order will send shockwaves through local authority planning, as councils have to redesign their development control policies and sometimes their whole approach to new business development. Some of the old restrictive policies may not be missed, but one likely consequence of the new Order is that, as local planning authorities (LPAs) find themselves more constrained in what they are empowered to control, they will be less willing to grant consent for changes of use when these carry with them wide-ranging freedoms under the new use classes, and when restrictive user conditions are clearly unwelcome to the Secretary of State for the Environment (SSE).

Some of the effects of the 1987 Order will be felt immediately, as owners and users of land seek to confirm their new freedoms by applying for the removal of restrictive user conditions and clauses, and for Section 53 determinations etc. But the changes on the ground will probably take effect only gradually, as leases fall in, buildings and sites come up for re-appraisal, and the property market adjusts to the new situation. Some local planning policies and practices may change quickly, but others will be re-assessed gradually in the light of experience with the new Order.

Robert Home
London
August 1987

Introduction
to Second Edition

The interest in, and changes brought about by, the 1987 Use Classes Order have been so great that I found myself preparing the second edition of this book only a year after the publication of the first. This edition adds to rather than takes away from the previous one, and fortunately I have had few mistakes to correct (the main one relates to taxi operators' offices). The main changes and additions in this edition:

- reflect the importance of the B1 class by enlarging the section on the B classes into a separate chapter which includes the results of recent research and relevant appeal decisions and policy changes;
- make some additions to the historical and case law sections and to the sources;
- update the text with significant appeal decisions, planning policy changes both local and central, and the relevant parts of the 1988 General Development Order, with the expansion of the sections on the A classes into a separate chapter;
- add a chapter on the new 1989 Use Classes Order for Scotland, and some material on UCOs in other countries.

Robert Home
London
February 1989

Acknowledgements

I would like to thank the following for their help in writing this book:

Eric Shapiro, BSc, FRICS, FRVA, FCIArb (senior partner of Moss Kaye and Roy Frank), who encouraged me to write this book and was always quick and willing to comment on my material from his wealth of experience in the property business;

Michael Crush, MA, FRICS, who made his encyclopaedic knowledge of development control and planning law freely available to me;

Tony Mason and Bob Roberts, who helped me over some frustrating moments while I grappled with intransigent new technology;

Ted Maloney and the other staff at the Duncan House library of North East London Polytechnic, who were willing 'gofers' (as always) in tracking down some of the obscurer source materials;

my wife Olive, who tolerated me during the months when I was infected by the use classes virus.

The idea of this book came from a conference on the Order which I chaired at the Café Royal in April 1987. I would therefore also like to thank Patricia Connelly, of Henry Stewart Conference Studies, for organising such a successful conference, and my fellow platform speakers, from whom I learned much: Andrew Beer of Wilde Sapte, Colin Bell of Grimley and Son, Ian Campbell of Campbell Gordon, James Donald of Strutt and Parker, Christopher Katkowski of 2 Paper Buildings, Temple, Richard Taylor of Fuller Peiser, and Michael Wilcox of Grimley and Son.

Abbreviations

DC	Development control
DCPN	Development control policy note
DOE	Department of the Environment
EUC	Established Use Certificate
GDO	Town and Country Planning General Development Order
GPM	Government Proposals to Modernise the UCO (1986)
LPA	Local Planning Authority
MHLG	Ministry of Housing and Local Government
PAG	Property Advisory Group (1985)
PCR	Property and Compensation Reports
PD	Permitted development
PPG	Planning Policy Guidance
RICS	Royal Institution of Chartered Surveyors
RTPI	Royal Town Planning Institute
SI	Statutory Instrument
SIUC	Special Industrial Use Class
SSE	Secretary of State for the Environment
TCP Act	Town and Country Planning Act
UCO	Town and Country Planning (Use Classes) Order

Chapter 1

The Use Classes Orders Before the Reform

The UCO and the GDO are important regulations for the planning system because they define large categories of land use and development which are free from planning control by local authorities. Also, being statutory instruments, they can be changed by the SSE without the procedural complexities and Parliamentary time that changes to primary legislation require. The Conservative government since 1979 has made several changes to the GDO, with the aim of reducing the scope of the planning system and freeing much private development from planning control, and the 1987 UCO applies the same approach.

UCOs have existed since the nationalisation of development rights under the 1947 TCP Act. They define categories of use which are 'not development', and therefore have the effect that, where planning permission exists for a use which falls within any use class, that use can be changed to any other use within the same use class without any further planning permission being necessary, unless conditions restricting change of use have been imposed by the LPA. Established uses of land (i.e. with a certificate of established use under section 94 of the 1971 TCP Act) have the same rights.

The main statutory provision for the UCO at present is in section 22(2)(f) of the TCP Act 1971 (formerly section 12(2)(f) of the 1947 Act). Section 22 defines what is and what is not development for the purposes of the Act, and thereby what requires planning permission. 'Development' is defined in section 22(1) as being:

'the carrying out of building, engineering, mining or other operations in, on, over or under land, or the making of any material change in the use of any building or other land.'

Section 22(2) goes on to state:

'The following operations or uses of land shall not be taken for the purposes of this Act to involve development of the land', and defines six such categories:

(a) minor building works of 'maintenance, improvement or other alteration' not materially affecting the external appearance of the building,

(b) highway maintenance work,

(c) inspection and repairs to underground services,

(d) 'the use of any buildings or other land within the curtilage of a dwellinghouse for any purpose incidental to the enjoyment of the dwellinghouse as such';

(e) 'the use of any land for the purposes of agriculture or forestry (including afforestation) and the use for any of those purposes of any building occupied together with land so used';

(f) 'in the case of buildings or other land which are used for a purpose of any class specified in an order made by the Secretary of State under this section, the use thereof for any other purpose of the same class'.

These categories, being not development, do not require planning permission from the LPA, should be immune from enforcement action, and indeed are outside the operation of the TCP Act altogether. Thus the use classes are particularly important to owners and users of land in defining the freedom with which they can use it without needing planning permission.

The categories in section 22(2), and therefore the classes in the UCO, are quite separate and distinct from the classes of permitted development for which the Secretary of State has granted deemed planning permission under the GDO, although (as will be seen) permitted development and the use classes are becoming more closely inter-related than previously.

HISTORY OF THE UCO 1948–72

The first UCO was passed in 1948, but the origins of the use classes can be traced to the so-called Model Clauses under the TCP Act 1932. Under that Act the Minister was authorised to issue Model Clauses to assist the local planning authority in preparing draft planning schemes (which preceded the bringing of all land under planning control in 1947). Such Model Clauses were issued in 1935 and amended in 1937, 1938 and 1939, after being referred to the Advisory Committee which the Minister had set up.

With the creation of a national planning framework under the 1947 TCP Act, the identification of use classes was important for defining the existing development rights in land. Two UCOs were passed in 1948, identical in content but different in purpose, both dated 5 May 1948 and coming into force on the first appointed day (1 July 1948). The one which is the ancestor of UCOs down to the present day was SI 1948, No. 954, passed under the provisions of section 12(2) of the TCP Act 1947. The other (SI 1948, No. 955), still in force because it was intended to be irrevocable, was specifically concerned with compensation matters (dealt with below), and is set out in

Appendix B. It was made under para. 6 of the Third Schedule of the 1947 Act (now para. 6 of the Eighth Schedule of the 1971 Act), and its amendment or revocation was prohibited under a proviso to section 111(4) of the 1947 Act, the reason being that valuation for planning compensation claims had to be made on fixed assumptions.

SI 954 was soon changed by the 1950 UCO (SI 1950, No. 1131), which came into force on 21 July 1950. This was a precursor to current deregulation measures because it reduced the number of classes and so liberalised the use class provisions. As the accompanying circular (no. 94, of 1950) said, it:

> 'represents a further step in the simplification of planning procedure. The amalgamation of certain of the Use Classes specified in the 1948 Order will allow a wider range of changes of use to take place without involving "development" for the purposes of the Act, and therefore without requiring planning permission or payment of development charge.'

The number of use classes was reduced from 22 to 18, but in other respects the 1950 UCO tightened control. The specific changes (some of which reappear as issues in the 1987 UCO) were as follows:

(i) the definitions of 'shop' and 'office' were amended in order to clarify the line of division between Classes I and II;

(ii) the scope of Class V was extended to take account of the Alkali etc. Works Order 1950;

(iii) the former Class X ('wholesale warehouse') and XI ('repository') were combined in one class;

(iv) hostels were no longer grouped with hotels, boarding houses and residential clubs 'in view of the wide range of uses covered by this term' (they were reunited in the 1987 UCO);

(v) the institutional uses formerly included in Classes XIII, XV, XVII and XVIII were grouped in two classes, XIV and XVI, 'the former including the generality of such uses and the latter those which demand particular care in the sitting (e.g. mental hospitals), boarding schools and residential colleges were placed in a separate class (XIII, changed by the 1987 UCO):

(vi) the uses formerly included in Classes XIX, XX, XXI and XXII were regrouped in two classes, XVII and XVIII.

The 1950 UCO remained in force for 13 years, apart from two minor amendment orders in 1960 (SI 1960 No. 282 with effect from 24 February 1960, and SI 1950 No. 1761 with effect from 27 September 1960). The first amendment UCO excluded the sale of motor vehicles from the scope of Class I (an exclusion which has been preserved in the 1987 UCO). As the accompanying Circular 10/60 stated:

'In making this amendment the Minister is concerned primarily with the effects which these changes of use may have on road traffic and, in certain circumstances, on local amenity. It is not his intention that unnecessary restrictions should be placed on the development of the motor trade in response to public demand. Accordingly, he asks planning authorities to examine proposals strictly on their merits, and to withhold permission only if satisfied that the particular proposal is objectionable on traffic grounds or for some other substantial reason.'

An amendment to the GDO at the same time made it unnecessary to obtain specific permission for a change from use for car sales back to shop use. The second amendment UCO in 1960 concerned betting offices (excluded from the definition of offices) and Classes V-VII, IX and XVI.

Under the 1962 TCP Act the 1950 and 1960 UCOs were revoked and replaced by the consolidated 1963 UCO (SI 1963 No. 708), with effect from 29 March 1963. A minor amendment followed in 1965 (SI 1965 No. 229), restoring a separation that formerly existed between Classes XVIII and XIX (assembly and sporting uses), but which has been again abandoned in the 1987 UCO assembly and leisure class.

The 1972 UCO replaced the 1963 UCO, under the then newly consolidated 1971 TCP Act. The main amendments made were:

(i) exclusion of launderettes, cafés and restaurants from the definitions of shop,

(ii) the recasting of Special Industrial Groups A, B and C;

(iii) the omission of the former Class XVI (use as a hospital, mental institution, prison or probation centre)

(vi) minor changes of wording in classes XVI, XVII and XVIII.

(v) omission of leather dresser, parchment maker and tanner from Class IX;

(vi) minor changes of wording in classes XVI, XVII and XVIII.

The 1972 UCO was both a restrictive and a deregulatory measure, increasing control in some areas and relaxing it in others. As its accompanying circular (97/72) stated:

'Account has been taken of increasing public concern about the freedom to establish certain kinds of premises under the previous Orders without development being involved. Accordingly, the present Order excludes certain uses from particular Use Classes (e.g. in the case of restaurants, cafés, snack bars and launderettes by amending the definition of "shop"; in the case of shops for the sale of hot food, by substituting this expression for "fried fish shop"; and by amending the definition of shop; in the case of amusement arcades by omitting the reference to a building for indoor games in new Class XVIII and substituting "sports hall"). The new order also takes account of some changes in attitude and of modern processes which justify minor relaxations (e.g. in bringing together all kinds of hospital in a single class, and by deleting leather making from Class IX). The special industrial classes have been regrouped taking account of the character of offence likely to arise from the process, rather that relying wholly on the criterion whether the works are registrable under the Alkali etc. Works Orders. Other changes have been made for the purpose of clarifying the position (e.g. in the definition of shops and offices).'

The 1972 UCO remained in force for fifteen years, until the major reform introduced by the 1987 UCO which is the subject of this book. A minor amendment in 1983 (SI 1983 No. 1614) excluded hazardous substances, and recent legislation has created a separate regime of control for such uses. Apart from that amendment, the 1972 UCO has lasted longer than any previous UCO without alteration, at a time of major changes in the economy and property industry and in attitudes to planning control and government regulation in general. It is, therefore, not surprising that the proposals to modernise it, which culminated in the 1987 UCO, were generally welcomed by those concerned with the planning system, even if the extent of the eventual reform created controversy.

CASE LAW ON USE CLASSES

The UCOs have given rise to case law as planning decisions get challenged in the High Court. While, as Judge Hodgson said in the case of *Forkhurst* v. *SSE* (1983), section 22(2)(f) has attracted relatively little case law compared with the wealth of judgments on other aspects of planning legislation, the design of the UCO has influenced the interpretation by the courts of the statutory formula of 'material change of use'. Certain principles relating to the UCO have emerged from the case law over the years.

(1) The impact of the UCO is to be assessed against the predominant use of the planning unit, not merely some ancillary or incidental use.
The main cases here are *Vickers Armstrong Ltd* v. *Central Land Board* (1958) *G. Percy Trentham* v. *Gloucestershire County Council* (1966) and *Brazil Concrete* v. *Amersham Rural District Council* (1967). Harrods Store was used to exemplify the principle by Lord Denning in the *Brazil Concrete* case:

'Take, for instance, Harrods Store. The unit is the whole building. The greater part is used for selling goods: but some parts are used for ancillary purposes, such as for offices and for packing articles for dispatch. The character of the whole is determined by its primary use as a shop. It is within Class I of the Use Classes Order. The ancillary use of part as an office does not bring it within Class II: and the ancillary use of part for packing does not make it a light industrial building within Class III.'

In other words, a use which is ordinarily incidental to a particular predominant use, but which appears as a different use in the UCO, can still be an incidental use (as Article 3(2) of the 1987 UCO states and previous UCOs have stated).

In the *Forkhurst* case Judge Hodgson said:
'The steps that have to be taken in deciding whether the use of land comes within a particular class are, I think, clear. First one has to arrive at an accurate description of the actual use; secondly, one has to see, as a matter of construction, whether the description fits into a use class; thirdly, one has to see whether description includes activities that fit into more than one use class; and fourthly, one has to decide whether, when there are activities that fit into more than one use class, the one is ordinarily incidental to the other.

A primary use of land cannot, however, be stretched unreasonably. As Lord Widgery CJ said (quoted in *Brooks and Burton* v. *SSE* (1978)):

'I do not believe, however, that it is possible for a piece of land to acquire, as it were, industrial rights for planning purposes merely because in one corner there is a tiny building used for industrial purposes.'

(2) The UCO should be interpreted restrictively: specified classes should not be stretched to accommodate activities which do not clearly fall within them.

It was established in several cases that a particular use could be *sui generis* and therefore falling outside any use class. In the *Brazil Concrete* case (1967) a builders' yard was held to be a *sui generis* use. In *Tessier* v. *SSE* (1976) a dutch barn had been used, first as a sculptor's studio, then for the repair and maintenance of motor vehicles. When an enforcement notice was served alleging a material change of use and upheld on appeal, the appellant sought to prove that both uses were industrial processes and therefore within Class IV (general industry). In his judgment Lord Widgery CJ referred to:

'... the danger of proliferation of industrial uses in residential areas unless a relatively severe construction is imposed on the terms of the Use Classes Order... I would follow that up by indicating the desirability of not stretching the Use Classes Order to embrace activities which do not clearly fall within it, because it is no bad thing that unusual activities should be treated as *sui generis* for this purpose.'

Article 3(6) of the 1987 Order extends this principle to *sui generis* uses.

(3) Use class rights can be restricted by conditions on a planning permission.

This had been stated from the earliest UCO in circulars starting with No. 42 in 1948, but was only tested in the courts in *City of London Corporation* v. *SSE and Another* (1972), on the validity of a condition which restricted the use of a building to a single named activity. In that case a planning application to change the use of part of the ground floor of premises, formerly used for textile wholesales and as a warehouse, to an employment agency was granted consent on appeal, but with a condition restricting the permitted use to that of an employment agency. The local planning authority (not the appellant) applied to quash the SSE's decision, contending that the condition was *ultra vires*, but failed. Citing the case of *Pyx Granite Co, Ltd* v. *MHLG* (1958), Judge Talbot found that:

'The essential elements are, first, that any condition must relate to and be directed to the fulfilment of planning policy, and, secondly, that it must fairly and reasonably relate to the permitted development...

The power [i.e. to make conditions restricting a use which would not amount to development] would seem to me necessary so that the planning authorities can meet the varied and particular circumstances of the planning of a particular area, and in my view this power does not go beyond the acts. In this case I can see the force of giving a planning authority the power to limit a use for office purposes to the use for a particular office use and this seems to me to be the essence of good planning. Furthermore, to limit the use to a particular office use relates directly to the development or use permitted and relates to it fairly and reasonably. To decide otherwise would, in my opinion, impose a fetter on the powers of planning authorities which is not found in the acts.'

In the *Carpet Decor Guildford (Ltd)* v. *SSE and Guildford Borough Council* case (1981) it was held that, if a planning authority wished to restrict the operation of the UCO or the GDO, then it must be done explicitly, i.e. by specific reference, and not by a loosely worded condition such as 'no variation from the deposited plans shall be made without the consent of the local planning authority'.

(4) The purpose of the UCO is not to define certain kinds of development, but the converse.

Change from one use to another in the same use class involves no development, but it does not follow that development will necessarily occur if a change is made to a use in another class. This was established in the case of *Rann and Another* v. *SSE and Another* (1979), a case of some importance in the reform of the UCO. It was cited in the PAG report which led to the 1987 UCO as demonstrating that the UCO 'is, by its very nature, a means of allowing freedom from, and not strengthening or formalising, statutory control' (para. 2.05). In the *Rann* case a house with permission as a hotel/guest house attracted an enforcement notice when it was used to provide holiday accommodation for mentally handicapped persons. Permission for change of use to a use within Class XIV of the 1972 UCO had been refused, and the SSE's decision upholding the enforcement notice considered the accommodation of mental patients to be akin to an institutional use, and materially different from a hotel/guest house use. Sir Douglas Frank QC, however, quashed the SSE's decision, stating in his judgment that:

> 'the Order of 1972 is being borrowed in this case for a purpose for which it was not intended. Its intended purpose is to put outside the ambit of the Act a change of use that has taken place within the same use class... Thus, if the Secretary of State is right, a guest-house providing holidays solely for children could be changed to a hospital or a home for the mentally sick without the grant of planning permission. I can think of a number of examples of such guest-houses — residential sailing and riding schools and mountaineering and physical education centres. The inquisitive bystander would be surprised to hear such places described as homes or institutions, and, if he were a neighbour, he might be dismayed to know that a planning permission would not be required to change the use to, say, a home for alcoholics.
>
> I do not think that Class XIV bears the extensive meaning ascribed to it by the Secretary of State. I think it is inherent in the words used that the care and maintenance referred to is of a special nature ... The basic feature of a guest-house as the word is used in the English language, however, is that it contains a transient population because it is there to serve people travelling who require short stays only ... I hold that the Secretary of State wrongly construed the use in this case as falling within Class XIV of the Order of 1972.'

As well as the issue of material change of use, this case also influenced the introduction of the new definition of care and the new residential institutions class (C2) in the 1987 UCO.

(5) Intensification of a use which falls within a use class will not require planning permission.

The reasoning here is that, although the change may amount to a material change, that change is deemed not to amount to 'development' under section 22(2)(f) of the 1971 TCP Act unless it is so great as to take the use outside its use class altogether. This was established in the *Brooks and Burton* case (1978), which was the only other case apart from *Rann* to be cited in the PAG report leading up to the 1987 UCO. The PAG report regarded it as 'the principal case on intensification' (PAG 1985, para. 12.01). In this case, which went to the Court of Appeal, a site had planning permission for light industrial purposes (Class III), but a concrete block-making and batching plant attracted an enforcement notice as a material change of use beyond Class III, and the SSE upheld the notice on appeal. The appellants claimed that the actual use was Class IV (general industrial), not Class III, and the judgment in the Court of Appeal stated:

'... the whole of the block-making site had been a "general industrial building" for the purposes of the Order of 1972 and so long as the appellant company confined their operations on the site to Class IV uses they were entitled to the benefit of section 22(2)(f) of the Act of 1971 even though any new processes and intensification of use amounted to a material change of use ... Intensification of use can be a material change of use. Whether it is or not depends upon the degree of intensification. Matters of degree are for the Secretary of State to decide.'

(In this case the court also took a side-swipe at planning in saying that it 'shares the antipathy of the Divisional Court for the degree of technicality into which the law of town and country has now come'. That was, however, a mild rebuke compared with the words of an earlier judge, in the case of *Britt* v. *Buckinghamshire County Council* (1962), who said:

'Hard indeed are the paths of local authorities in striving to administer the town and country planning legislation of recent years ... It is a subject which stinks in the noses of the public and not without reason.')

Before *Brooks and Burton Ltd* v. *SSE* (1978), several cases on intensification had concerned an increase in the number of caravans on a caravan site. Finding that no intensification affecting the character of the land that taken place, Judge Salmon, in *Glamorgan* v. *Carter* (1962), expressed the opinion that:

'once it is established that the whole site is used as a caravan site it does not seem to me that the use is materially changed by bringing a larger number of caravans upon the site.'

In *Guildford* v. *Fortescue* (1959) an increase from eight caravans to 27 was held not to involve development. Thus, once a use has become established as the sole use of a site it is doubtful whether an increase in the intensity of that use alone can constitute development. But the courts have been careful not to rule out the possibility, for in *Guildford Rural District Council* v. *Fortescue* (1959) Lord Evershed MR expressed reservations about the contention that mere intensity of use could never be relevant:

'If the Kennington Oval Cricket Ground were used so as to provide continuously a greater number of pitches, on which boys or others could contemporaneously play cricket during the summer, no doubt the Kennington Oval would remain a cricket ground but it would be a cricket ground materially changed: it would no longer be a first-class county cricket ground but would be a cricket ground of a different kind. It is also, as it seems to me, obvious that increasing intensity of use or occupation may involve a substantial increase in the burden of the services which a local authority has to supply, and that, in truth, might, in some cases at least, be material in considering whether the use of the land had been materially changed.'

The interpretation of intensification will be affected by the new statutory provisions on sub-division in the Housing and Planning Act 1986.

A generally less tolerant view of intensification has been applied to residential uses, and the 1987 UCO makes it clear that sub-division of dwelling-houses is still development. In circular 67 of 1949 the Minister gave as examples of changes in the 'degree' of existing use a change from private residence to guest-house, lodging-house or hotel. In *Birmingham Corporation* v. *Habib Ullah* (1964), for instance, the change of use of a single dwelling house to a house let in lodgings (now more usually referred to as multiple paying occupation) was held to be material. In that case Lord Parker CJ concentrated on the character of the land:

'The matter, however, is I think made clear by the Town and Country Planning (Use Classes) Order ... itself. Class I of that Order is dealing with "use as a shop for any purpose except as a fried fish shop" etc. That is clearly contemplating that the fact that the premises remain a shop after the alleged change is not conclusive, but that you must consider the purpose for which the shop has been used, whether the purpose has changed. The same is to be found in Class II, "use as an office for any purpose" and, of course, Class XI ... "use as a boarding or guest house, a residential club, or a hotel providing sleeping accommodation", all of which can loosely be called residential or houses where people dwell, and yet this contemplates that but for the Order there would be a development by a change of use of the house from one purpose to its use for another.'

(6) The ability to switch between permitted uses cannot be exploited by 'minimal' implementation of a consent.

In the case of *Kwik Save Discount Group* v. *SSE* (1981) permission had been granted for a self-service petrol station and car showroom. The plaintiffs acquired the site before the buildings had been occupied and wished to use them immediately as a retail store. To claim the benefit of the UCO they first used the premises for one month as a car showroom, offering five cars for sale. The Court Appeal upheld the SSE's ruling that such a use was minimal, and insufficient to establish a starting point for exploitation of the Order. The current wording of the UCO ('where a building or other land is used') presupposes that a planning permission must first be implemented and the use commenced before advantage may be taken of use class rights.

(7) Use for a trade or business did not require the making of profit or indeed carrying on a commercial activity.

The case of *Rael-Brook Ltd v. MHLG* (1967) addressed the question of whether the making of profit or carrying on of a commercial activity was essential in order that a process might be carried on in the course of trade or business. In that case a building formerly used for cooking school meals was taken over for a light industrial use, the company arguing successfully that both fell within Class III (light industry). The then Judge Widgery said:

'There are a great many enthusiastic amateur engineers who have workshops in which they tune motor cars and carry out all manner of processes which are concerned with the making, altering, repairing, ornamenting or finishing of some article, and a serious proliferation of industrial activity in residential areas might follow if all such workshops could be turned over to commercial industrial activity without any control by the planning authority. Counsel's arguments in this case both recognise that the broad distinction desired to be drawn is that between the amateur and the professional, but it does not follow that commercial motives provide the final or only test.'

The reserved judgment of the court in that case was that:

'neither the making of profit nor any commerical activity was essential for a process to be "carried on in the course of trade or business" within the meaning of article 2(2) of the Town and Country Planning (Use Classes) Order 1950, and a local authority's activity exhibiting all the possible features of a business other than the making of profit or any commercial activity was not excluded. Accordingly, since the provision of school meals was an occupation as distinguished from pleasure, and was a continuous and serious undertaking earnestly pursued in fulfilling a duty, the existing use of the building on the company obtaining possession was a use within class III'.

This case could be relevant to the planning status of public authority land and buildings as public services are progressively privatised.

(8) Where one use within a class is the subject of a successful enforcement notice, it is not permissible to change from another permitted use in the class to that use.

This followed the case of *St. Hermans Estate Co. Ltd v. Havant and Waterloo UDC* (1971), where an ingenious argument was unsuccessfully mounted that a use prohibited in an enforcement notice (relating to manufacturing of concrete blocks and slabs) could be resumed because another use on the site within the same use class (in this case Classes III and IV of the UCO) had established use rights, and a change of use did not require planning permission.

RELATION TO OTHER REGULATIONS

Planning control is exercised in combination with a range of other licensing controls, usually administered by the public health authority or the magistrates. These include (to mention but a few) licensing under the Caravan Sites Act 1960, licensing of public houses and gaming establishments, and registration of houses in multiple occupation. The principle that has been followed, as stated in PPG1 (formerly DCPN1), is this:

'22. Moreover, planning legislation should not normally be used to secure objects achievable under other legislation. For example, planning permission for a betting office should not be refused on moral grounds or because it is considered that there are sufficient such uses in the area already. The Gaming Acts provide for licensing of betting offices, *inter alia* on the basis of the demand from place to place.

As will be seen, the 1987 UCO seems to be departing from this principle in the cause of deregulation.

Development orders made under section 24 of the 1971 TCP Act may grant a general permission for certain types of development (permitted development — PD), without any need for a prospective developer to make a planning application. A general order (GDO) will apply to all land, with a special order applying to specified land or descriptions of land. Local authorities can also withdraw PD rights through the mechanism of a direction under Article 4 of the GDO, once confirmed by the SSE, but compensation may be payable.

Class III of the GDO schedule of PD, now Part 3 of the 1988 GDO, deals with changes of use. For many years change of use to a light industrial building from a general industrial building, and to a shop from any of the exclusions in Class I (i.e. fried fish shop, tripe shop, shop for the sale of pet animals and birds, cats-meat shop, or shop for sale of motor vehicles) have been permitted development under this class of the GDO. The 1981 GDO added to the categories in Class III change to a light industrial building from a warehousing (Class X) use, and change to Class X from light or general industrial, but only in respect of premises not exceeding 235 square metres floorspace. The 1988 GDO retained these freedoms and made further changes.

COMPENSATION

Compensation is outside the scope of this book, but can arise in use classes cases through the 1948 UCO (reproduced in Appendix B) and the Eighth Schedule of the 1971 TCP Act. The 1947 TCP Act established a set of exemptions from the development charge, which were regarded as falling within the existing use of the land but nevertheless might still require planning permission. Refusal or conditional grant of permission for these exemptions could involve the LPA in liability to compensate, because existing use rights had been interfered with. Among the categories of development ranking for compensation under section 169 of the 1971 TCP Act as set out in Part II of the Eighth Schedule, is the following:

'In the case of a building or other land which, at a material date (i.e. the first appointed day, 1 July 1948) was used for a purpose within any general class specified in the Town and Country Planning (Use Classes for Third Schedule Purposes) Order 1948, or which having been unoccupied on and at all times since the first appointed day, was last used (otherwise than before 7 January 1937) for any purpose, the use of that building or land for any other purpose falling within the same general class.'

Thus, if a building or land was used in 1948 for one purpose within a particular use class (e.g. as a hostel under Class XIV of the 1948 UCO), then compensation would be payable on refusal for a change of use which had been subsequently removed from that class. One example would be a change of use between a hotel and a hostel, which in 1948 were both in Class XIV, but from which class hostel was subsequently removed.

Such cases are very few and far between, and would require careful research to establish the use at the first appointed day, and there seem to have been no such examples of compensation paid in recent years. Another paragraph of the Schedule, however, that relating to enlargement of a building by a tenth, was the subject of the celebrated case of *Peaktop Properties* v. *Camden LBC* (1983). In that case a developer obtained £100,000 compensation from the London Borough of Camden following refusal of permission for an enlargement by adding penthouses to a block of flats. The TCP (Compensation) Act 1985 closed that particular compensation loophole, and at the same time the House of Lords secured an undertaking from the Government to review all the compensation provisions of the TCP Act.

It now seems likely that the compensation provisions of the 1948 GDO and section 169 will be repealed, although the 1948 UCO will still remain as the basis of compensation in appropriate cases following compulsory purchase or purchase notices. The Government's 1986 consultation paper on compensation, following the House of Lords' debates, set out the following principles as an appropriate basis for compensation:

'(a) planning permission should normally be granted unless there are sound, relevant and clearly stated reasons why it should not be;

(b) since the Town and Country Planning Act 1947, all development as defined in the Act has been subject to planning control; with the lapse of time since the introduction of the system, it is now practicable to operate on the general principle for all forms of development that compensation should not be payable when permission to undertake development is refused or when general permission is rescinded (apart from cases in the pipeline when the change is made);

(c) where planning permission has been given for a development either generally or upon application, compensation should be paid if permission is taken away in a particular case but not generally.' (Planning Compensation 1986, para. 2)

The repeal of section 169 will prevent possible abuse in the circumstances that the compensation paper recognised:

'An unscrupulous developer has little to lose from submitting an application for planning permission for development which is clearly unacceptable under normal planning criteria, with the hope that a refusal will lead to a substantial compensation agreement. In the case of the "penthouse flats" applications which led to the passing of the 1985 Act there was a significant number of applications which were not pursued once planning permission had been granted. While the Department has no evidence of other abuses of this kind it is clear that planning authorities are concerned about the possibility.' (Planning Compensation 1986, para. 16)

Chapter 2

The Reform of the Order 1985–7

The Conservative government, since 1979, has been committed to preserving the planning system, but also to reducing what it sees as the bureaucratic burdens of planning control. The UCO remained untouched in the early reforms which modified the GDO, introduced enterprise zones and made other minor amendments to the system, but in the second Conservative administration (1983–7) the continuing pressure for deregulation targeted the UCO as an important area needing reform. In 1984 the Royal Institution of Chartered Surveyors highlighted the UCO as an obstacle to 'high-tech' developments in particular (RICS 1984a).

The 1987 UCO is, therefore, one of the fruits of a major Government deregulation initiative which was launched in the White Paper, *Lifting the Burden* (Command 9571), presented to Parliament in July 1985. This included proposals for reducing the bureaucratic burdens on business in town and country planning, transport, customs and excise, agriculture and other areas of Government regulation. As the White Paper said in para 3.1:

'The town and country planning system has not changed in its essentials since it was established in 1947. In many ways it has served the country well and the Government has no intention of abolishing it. But it also imposes costs on the economy and constraints on enterprise that are not always justified by any real public benefit in the individual case. It can cause delay and uncertainty even where applications are eventually approved. Too often the very wide discretionary power that the system affords is used to apply excessively detailed and onerous controls of a kind that would not be tolerated in general legislation. If the system is to remain effective it must be used in a way that does not impose an unnecessary degree of regulation on firms and on individuals.'

At the same time as the White Paper the DOE issued a new circular on development and employment (14/85), which urged the planning system to 'respond positively and promptly to proposals for development ... unless that development would cause demonstrable harm to interests of acknowledged importance'. It also stressed the importance of helping small firms by avoiding 'unnecessarily onerous and complex controls'. The White Paper went on to propose the creation of Simplified Planning Zones (a development of the Enterprise Zone concept introduced in 1980), changes to the GDO, Advertisement Regulations, and the 1971 Act, simplified appeals procedures, and guidance on planning in relation to small firms. In para. 3.5(iii) it also announced a review of the UCO:

'The UCO enables land and buildings to be used for various purposes without the need for planning permission, and is thus a means of deregulation like the GDO. Unlike the GDO, however, the UCO has not been substantially changed since it was first introduced in 1948, and is clearly overdue for review in the light of today's conditions. In particular, it needs to take account of the requirements of the typical "high tech" firms where manufacturing offices, research and development, warehousing and other activities may be carried on in a single building and where the mix of uses and space utilisation may need to be constantly changed and adapted to the needs of the business. Since the UCO is intended to permit and not restrict compatible uses, it is essential that it should be designed to do this effectively.' (Command 9571 1985, p.11)

The complex task of reviewing the UCO was entrusted to a sub-group of the Property Advisory Group of the Department of the Environment, which had existed for some years and produced occasional reports before on topics such as planning gain. The sub-group's brief was to undertake 'a wide-ranging and fundamental review of the Order, with the object of modernising and recasting it, within the basic framework of Part III of the 1971 Act, in the light of the circumstances and needs of the present and the foreseeable future'. The brief went on:

'4. The aim is to reduce the number of classes to the minimum compatible with keeping within specific control changes of use which, because of their environmental consequences or relationships to other uses, need to be subject to prior authority; to permit, without the need for specific application, changes in the proportion or "mix" of uses of different kinds within a single building; and, where possible, to permit change of use between use classes by changing from a more "noxious" type of use to a less noxious one (the "escalator" concept). Overall, the intention is to enable the occupiers of land and buildings to enjoy the maximum practical flexibility in the use of their property, free from public control.' (PAG 1985, Appendix B)

The sub-group was given a very tight schedule, being briefed in June 1985 to produce outline proposals by September 1985, and its report was finally made public on 2 December 1985. The speed with which it had to work inevitably meant that very little background research could be undertaken. Although the DOE annually commissions several million pounds' worth of contract research from outside organisations, little of this has been allocated to assess the need for and impact of a reform of the UCO which would clearly have wide-reaching implications for the planning system. Also the sub-group did not undertake any consultation process before producing its report, and there was some criticism that the DOE did not itself undertake the exercise.

The members of PAG in the sub-group were as follows:

Richard Caws CBE, FRICS (Chairman, senior partner of Debenham, Tewson and Chinnocks, chartered surveyors of London, and formerly involved with the Dobry Committee on the review of the development control system, 1973-5)

Mrs Honor Chapman BSc, MPhil, FRICS, MRTPI (partner and research director for Jones Lang Wootton, chartered surveyors of London, formerly a partner in the firm of Nathaniel Lichfield and Associates, town planning consultants)

Geoffrey Powell FRICS, FSVA, ACIArb (former senior partner of Gerald Eve & Co., chartered surveyors of London, chairman of the Property Advisory Group, also member of British Railways Property Board, deputy chairman of the Local Government Boundary Commission for England)

Derek Wood QC (barrister, PAG member since 1978, and a former Labour councillor in the London Borough of Bromley).

In addition Nigel Mobbs (Chairman and Chief Executive of Slough Estates, a former president of the British Property Federation, and of the Association of British Chambers of Commerce) was appointed by the DOE to serve on the sub-group, with Mr W. Mackenzie OBE (Group Managing Director of Slough Estates) serving as an alternate. Mr W.H. Alexander was Secretary to the sub-group.

As can be seen from the list of members, only one member of the sub-group was a professional planner, and she had formerly been a private consultant, not in local government. There was no senior planner from local government to advise on the practical implications of the proposed changes for planning control, a role which was left to the Royal Town Planning Institute and other planning organisations in commenting on the report after it was produced. Critics of the subsequent report, including the RTPI, claimed it was biased in favour of developers and owners of property, and gave scant attention to the concerns of tenants, users, neighbours and indeed the public as a whole. Some of the difficulties that may be encountered in the application of the 1987 UCO can be attributed to these limitations of the sub-groups's composition.

The sub-group set to work with a will, and, recognising the political context of its investigation, saw the UCO as:

'essentially a de-regulatory instrument. In a wide range of cases it frees occupiers or potential occupiers of land or buildings who wish materially to change the use to which the property is currently being put from the necessity of applying for planning permission. The Group is nevertheless aware that the view is erroneously held in some quarters, and even by some professional planners, that a change of use from one class to another must constitute development. This mistaken view was rejected by the Courts in *Rann* ... To look at the UCO in this erroneous way is to run the risk of transforming it from a liberalising into a restrictive measure. We consider it important to emphasise in this Report that the UCO is, by its very nature, a means of allowing freedom from, and not strengthening or formalising statutory control.' (PAG 1985, para. 2.05)

Rann was one of only two legal cases referred to in the PAG Report, both supporting a deregulatory argument. The other case, *Brooks and Burton* (1978), was used to support the argument that intensification of use cannot be applied to a use falling within a use class.

The sub-group did not shrink from a radical approach, given its brief to undertake a 'fundamental' review, and was prepared to consider (paras. 4.03–9) the fundamental question of whether a change of use need require planning permission at all. It concluded, however, that planning control over the use of land was needed for two main reasons:

'(1) to protect the living and working conditions and the general environment of the public at large, or of individuals or groups from intrusive and objectionable change;

(2) to ensure that certain essential land uses are established and maintained in locations where they can be conveniently and appropriately carried on.'

The sub-group's views on the reasons why reform of the UCO were necessary are interesting in the light of the final outcome in the 1987 Order:

'4.02. In any case, and irrespective of the historical explanation for the present classification of some uses, major changes have taken place since 1948 in the distribution and nature of economic activity, which have altered the face of much of our planning. First, traditional industry has declined in most parts of the country, with an increase in the amount of vacant buildings as well as unemployment. At the same time, there has been a growth in the importance of service industry in many areas. Indeed, the different functions of production, administration and selling are often now being undertaken in the same building, particularly in what has been called "high technology" or "knowledge-based" industry, and the emergence of the American style of "business park". There have also been major shifts in population, with the contraction of metropolitan conurbations, and the growth of small towns and villages. A motorway network has been built, and much more use is now made of roads for goods and personal transport. This in turn is associated with major changes in retailing, with the decline of the traditional high street, and the growth of larger stores, and "out of town" centres. There are also changes in the size of activities, with the contraction of many larger firms, and some growth among smaller enterprises. All these factors indicate that the UCO needs to be brought up to date.' (PAG report 1985)

The sub-group did not depart from the long-established principle that planning should not be concerned with fluctuations in the value of individual property. It did, however, consider that:

'The planning system may be concerned tangentially with land values, however, in this way. A particular parcel of land, or a particular area, may be performing a particular function which it is in the interests of the public to retain, and the use of that land may be designated by the local planning authority accordingly. The effect of such a decision may be to hold the value below that which the land would otherwise attain. One example would be that of shops within a residential community. Another example is that of the land which is devoted to some specially noxious or anti-social purpose, such as the disposal of chemical waste, which must be carried out at a site which is isolated from other types of development. If the range of permissible uses of the land in question were widened, that might have the effect of driving up the market value of the land so that the current users of the land would be outbid by others. They might then be driven to relocate themselves at a less appropriate place, or perhaps face difficulty in re-establishing themselves at all. There would be, in our view, a limited number of cases in which this consideration would be relevant. In the majority of cases the property market will usually adjust readily to any changed framework.' (PAG 1985, para. 4.10)

As PPGI said:

'23. More generally, it is not the function of the planning system to interfere with or inhibit competition between users and investors in land, or to regulate the overall provision and character of space for particular uses for other than land-use planning reasons.'

The sub-group considered the possibility of geographical variations in the application of the UCO. The RTPI wanted some areas to keep more planning control over change of use, but the sub-group took the opposite view, that any local measures 'should build on, and not detract from, the UCO' (para. 5.05), and recommended that local planning authorities 'are given the fullest entitlement and encouragement to enlarge even further upon freedom to change use, both through the Simplified Planning Zones and Flexible Planning Permissions procedures.'

The PAG sub-groups's final report (PAG 1985) was a 64-page typescript (excluding appendices). Its 14 recommendations, set out in Appendix C of the report and in full in Appendix D of this book, amounted to a drastic and radical reshaping of the UCO. The main changes to the individual use classes are reproduced in Figure 1.

The PAG report was made public in December 1985, and comments were invited from interested parties, which resulted in many representations being made to the DOE. The response was mixed. Many people in the development industry were unaware that the review was being undertaken, such was the secrecy of the PAG deliberations, but most commentators agreed that change was long overdue. The two areas which attracted the most criticism were PAG's recommendations on home-based business activity and shopping areas. On both of these the Government declined the radical change proposed, although on a third contentious area, that of the new business class, it kept the recommendation unaltered.

On the first contentious recommendation, concerning home based economic activity, the PAG report said this:

'11.03 ... some business activities can fairly be described as "incidental to the enjoyment of the dwellinghouses as such". This will be especially the case if the activity in question is carried on privately by the occupier, working for example in a small workshop or a studio, or doing office work in a room set aside for that purpose. The giving of music lessons constitutes a classic problem. The dividing line between some hobbies and certain business activities is virtually non-existent. There are planning decisions on both sides of the line. The use of outbuildings for mending cloth, the carrying on of a tailoring business, dog breeding, the use of one room as a nursing agency, the use of premises as a veterinary operating theatre, and the use of a kitchen to prepare sandwiches and salads for local firms, have all been held to constitute development. By contrast, dog breeding at a house in one and a half acres of grounds, and the part time use of premises for a hairdressing business or as a furniture showroom have been held not to constitute development.'

The PAG report went on to recommend the creation of a new dwellinghouse class to include:

'the use of a building by any resident concurrently with his or her occupation of the property for any activity compatible with the principal use, which (1) can be carried on in any residential area without detriment to the amenity of that area by reason of noise, vibration, smell, fumes, smoke, soot, ash, dust or grit; (2) does not generate vehicular traffic of a type or amount which is detrimental to the amenity of the area in which it is conducted; and (3) does not involve the presence on the premises of more than five persons engaged in business (including the proprietors) at any one time.'

This proposal proved altogether too much to swallow, and attracted much hostile reaction. Residents in Marylebone and other parts of central London were concerned about the proliferation of businesses uses that would follow, and it is in an area of planning control where enforcement frequently occurs (Home, Bloomfield and Maclean 1985). The RICS had this to say:

'The proposal ... goes beyond the boundary of that which we believe to be acceptable in a wide range of circumstances encountered in practice. We also believe that it would be impossible to enforce the condition relating to traffic and that the detrimental effects on those living nearby could be quite considerable.' (RICS 1986a, para. 18)

The RTPI view was that:

'The only clear threshold is one that requires permission for non-residents to work in the home other than for purposes directly related to the residence. Applications can then be considered on their individual merits with full recognition of the factors of amenity, noise, traffic etc. In considering such applications, a useful indicator can be the proportion of the residence used for business purposes. This allows for the differential impact of the nature of the residential property eg. a large detached house in substantial grounds or a terrace house subdivided into one bedroom flats.' (RTPI 1986)

The Government did introduce a new dwellinghouse class in the 1987 UCO, but, bowing to the criticism of the home working aspect, omitted any reference to it, and confined itself instead to a new circular, 2/86, to clarify the position. This stated that planning permission for working at home 'is not usually needed where the use of part of a dwellinghouse for business purposes does not change the overall character of its use as a residence' (see also Walsh, Thomas and Porter 1986).

The second contentious proposal in the PAG report concerned retailing, where the sub-group recommended a major expansion of the definition of 'shop' to encompass 'certain types of office in which the activity carried on consists of the provision of personal services to the public' and also shops for the sale of hot food. The RICS in its comments had serious reservations about this proposal:

'We are particularly concerned about the effect the proposal might have on shop frontages. Without the need to apply for planning permission the

Fig. 1 — Schematic Relationship of Present to Proposed Use Classes (GPM 1986)

PRESENT USE CLASSES	USES	PROPOSED USE CLASSES
	* Restaurants, public houses, snack bars, cafés	
	* Shops for the sale of hot food	** *New prepared food class*
	* Shops for the sale of motor vehicles	
	* Shops for the sale of pets, cats meat or tripe	
CLASS I	Other shops for the sale of retail goods (including 'retail warehouses')	
	Hairdressers, undertakers, travel and ticket agencies, post offices, receivers of goods to be washed, cleaned or repaired	
	* Showrooms, buildings for the hiring out of domestic or personal goods or articles	*New retail class*
	* Betting offices	
CLASS II	Banks, building societies, estate and employment agencies	
	Professional services to the public (e.g. solicitors)	** *New financial and professional services class*
		— *New retail class* —
	Other offices	
CLASS III	Light industry †	
	* Research development, laboratories, studios, including film, television and sound recording studios	*New business class*
CLASS IV	General industry	*General industrial class (no change proposed)*
CLASSES V–IX	Special industrial groups	*Special industrial classes (to be the subject of a separate technical review)*
CLASS X	Wholesale warehouse or repository	*Warehousing class (no change proposed)*

⌐ ⌐ *Revised structure of classes proposed by Property Advisory Group sub-group*

▭ *Structure of classes proposed in this consultation paper*

* Currently *sui generis* (i.e. not in any use class)

** *One way movement to retail class to be permitted by GDO*

† Such as could be carried on in any residential area
without detriment to the amenity of the area by reason
of noise, vibration, smell, fumes, smoke, soot, ash, dust or grit

| CLASS XI | Hotels, boarding and guest houses, old persons homes not providing care and maintenance | |
| | | *Hotels etc. class* |

CLASS XII	Residential schools and colleges	
CLASS XIV	Hospitals and homes	*New residential institutions class (7 or more residents)*
	* Hostels *(may already be included in the classes above)*	
		(more than 10 residents)

	* Non-residential education and training centres	
CLASS XV	Clinics, health centres etc.	
CLASS XVI	Museums, public halls etc.	*New non-residential institutions class*

| CLASS XIII | Places of worship and church halls | *New non-residential institutions class* |

CLASS XVII	Theatres, cinemas, concert halls etc.	
CLASS XVIII	Dance and sports halls, baths etc.	
	* Other indoor and outdoor sports and leisure uses	*New assembly and leisure class*

* Dwellings

* Small businesses at home
(PAG sub-group proposed no more than 5 people engaged in any business activity to be present on the premises at any one time)
(Government proposes to leave the current requirements for planning permission unchanged: it has clarified these in a booklet for small businesses)

* Communal housing of elderly and handicapped
(PAG sub-group proposed up to 10 residents)
(Government proposes no more than 6 residents)   *New private residences class*

* Retail sales on open land   *New open land class*

* Light industry on open land   *New open land class*

* General industry on open land   *New open land class*

Government proposes all classes to include analogous uses of open land

* Currently *sui generis* (not in any use class)

balance within a shopping area as between retail outlets and those providing services rather than goods would have to be determined by market forces. Many outlets providing services prefer high street locations so as to benefit from the pedestrian flow generated by the purely retail outlets in the area. Although it is therefore unlikely that if left to the market a string of outlets providing services only would arise, the need to maintain the continuity of retail shopping frontages is vital if the liveliness of shopping areas is to be maintained. It is for this reason that we would only support proposed stage 4 if it expressly excluded ground floor shop premises and was thereby confined to upper floors.' (RICS 1986a)

The Government again bowed to pressure in keeping two separate classes for shops and financial/professional services. which PAG wanted to merge. On this aspect the GPM said this:

'13. The Government has considered these options very carefully in the light of the representations received. The character of a shopping centre depends on many factors such as size, location, access, number and range of shops and other facilities. The vitality of a shopping centre depends on the number of people it can attract and this will often be its main planning characteristic, together with the consequential vehicular and pedestrian traffic, and requirements for parking, loading and public transport facilities. Many local authorities have policies designed to maintain and strengthen the retail element in primary areas dominated by shops for the retail sale of goods. Adoption of either Stage 3 or Stage 4 of the sub-group recommendations would take away the ability of local planning authorities to implement these planning policies.' (GPM 1986).

1986: THE GOVERNMENT'S PROPOSALS

The large number of responses to PAG which the DOE had to consider, and which raised more complex issues than had at first been envisaged, meant that, when the second White Paper on deregulation, *Building Business ... Not Barriers* (Command 9794), was laid before Parliament in May 1986, the UCO was not part of the detailed proposals. It was a month later, in June 1986, that the DOE made public its 'Proposals to modernise the Town and Country Planning (Use Classes) Order 1972' (GPM 1986), a brief document of only seven pages and a diagram, published by the DOE itself, not through HMSO. The proposals were announced in the House of Lords on 16 June 1986 (Hansard 1986). Their stated aim (para. 5) was two-fold:

'First, to reduce the number of use classes to the minimum consistent with retaining effective control over changes of use which, because of environmental consequences or relationship with other uses, need to be subject to specific control; second, to ensure that the scope of each class is wide enough to take in changes of use which generally do not need to be subject to specific control.'

The GPM document did not accept all of the PAG recommendations, and summarised the main changes as follows:

'(i) separate use classes for shops and for premises from which financial or professional services are provided direct to the public visiting the premises (e.g. building societies and banks);

(ii) the creation of a new use class for premises used for the preparation and sale of food;

(iii) the introduction of a GDO freedom to permit both financial and professional services premises and hot food premises to become shops but not *vice-versa* without specific planning permission;

(iv) the creation of a new "business" class by merging light industrial uses with office uses other than those for financial and professional services provided direct to the public visiting the premises;

(v) no change to the current general and special industrial classes, Classes IV–IX, but a separate technical review of the latter leading to a later amendment of the Order;

(vi) no change to the current wholesale class, Class X;

(vii) the retention of the current separate use class covering uses as a hotel, or a boarding or guest house (including those residential homes where no special care or maintenance is provided);

(viii) the creation of a residential institutions class by merging the current Classes XII and XIV;

(ix) the creation of a new single "non-residential institutions" class covering the current Class XIII, XV and XVI, and including non-residential schools and colleges, and churches and church halls;

(x) the creation of an "assembly and leisure" class covering theatres, cinemas, music and concert halls, dance halls, and all indoor and outdoor sports and leisure uses;

(xi) the creation of a new "private residential" use class to include use as a dwellinghouse and use as a home provided that no more than 6 people are normally resident; the revised Order will not alter the current requirement that planning permission for working at home is needed if the overall character of the use of the premises as a residence would be changed;

(xii) the inclusion of uses of open land in the same class as the use of buildings for the same purpose;

(xiii) clarification that planning permission is not required to sub-divide non-residential buildings, provided that the existing use of the whole building and the proposed use of the parts fall within the same use class. (This proposal will require amendment of primary legislation.) Planning permission will continue to be required for the sub-division of dwellinghouses.'

A second round of public consultations followed, and elicited further representations, including a rearguard action by the RTPI. The final version of the Order, however, was little different from the GPM.

It was during this period of nearly a year between the GPM and the 1987 Order that the Government took the opportunity to incorporate one of the PAG recommendations, that on sub-division, into primary legislation. The Housing and Planning Act 1986 was passing through Parliament, which introduced simplified planning zones, a regime for controlling hazardous substances, and various other measures. Included in Part V of the Act were various miscellaneous provisions, linked to Schedule 11, the first paragraph of which stated:

'Operation of Use Classes Order on subdivision of planning unit
    1. In section 22(2) of the Town and Country Planning Act 1971 (operations and changes of use not amounting to development), in paragraph (f) (use of same prescribed class as existing use) for "the use thereof" substitute "the use of the buildings or other land or, subject to the provisions of the order, of any part thereof".'

The legal position on the sub-division of planning units had been somewhat uncertain, and had arisen in a number of cases, notably *Wakelin* v. *SSE* (1977), *Winton and Others* v. *SSE and Another* (1982) and *Brooks and Burton* (1977). The PAG report considered that any sub-division falling within the UCO, even if it brings about a material change of use, ought not to require planning permission:

'Looking at the matter from a purely practical point of view, it is desirable that occupiers of land should have maximum flexibility so that they can split up their property or amalgamate it into different units according to their own requirements from time to time, or the different demands which the market creates at different times, provided that no change in the basic use to which the building is put is involved' (PAG 1985, para. 12.08).

The GPM considered this 'an important proposal', saying:

'There would be considerable benefits for businesses if planning permission were no longer required for every change in the division of industrial or commercial premises. Speculatively built units could be occupied more quickly in cases where the floor area is not right for the prospective occupier, since there would be no need to delay while planning permission for a different division of the unit was sought.' (GPM 1986, para. 33).

The RTPI did not agree with this sweeping approach, being concerned at the effects of sub-division on servicing and parking, particularly where sub-division involved older industrial premises with high site coverage and inadequate loading and parking space. It argued that control over sub-division offered a degree of protection for adjacent occupiers, and recommended an alternative approach of making sub-division permitted development under the GDO, giving LPAs the option of seeking Article 4 directions. Without some control the RTPI said that traffic regulation orders might have to be made around sub-divided premises, forcing parking in adjacent residential areas. The RTPI view did not prevail, and the PAG approach was taken up in the 1986 Housing and Planning Act.

Having changed the primary legislation, the position on sub-division of dwellinghouses remained unclear. The PAG report had recommended that the sub-division of one separate dwelling into two or more dwellings should not be development, which would have required the repeal of section 22(3)(a) of the 1971 TCP Act. The GPM did not accept the recommendation, and the 1987 UCO (Article 4) now clarifies the position.

'In the case of a building used for a purpose within class C3 (dwellinghouses) in the Schedule, the use as a separate dwellinghouse of any part of the building is not, by virtue of this order, to be taken as not amounting to development;.'

FEBRUARY 1987: THE SAVILE ROW TAILORS' ADJOURNMENT DEBATE

The UCO proposals attracted very little interest from the opposition political parties and, not being primary legislation, consumed little Parliamentary time. The exception, however, was the resistance to the proposed business class put up by the 40 tailoring firms of Savile Row, who succeeded in getting an adjournment debate in the House of Commons on 5 February 1987, initiated by the MP for Westminster (North), Mr John Wheeler (Hansard 1987).

In his speech in the House of Commons, having mentioned the special connections of the Speaker of the House with the tailoring trade, Mr Wheeler went on to express concern at the possible increase in rental levels for tailoring premises which the proposed new business class could bring about:

'Public interest in amenity and the use of land is the kernel of this issue. The position that tailors occupy in London and their craft provides employment for some 3000 people who live and work in London and who contribute to the £27 million which the trade produces in the value of its products, but also to that vital £15 million a year which goes to overseas exports...

In the City of Westminster we have a mosaic of commercial activities which each relate to the other. Thus, people will stay in the hotels, visit the Oxford street retail sector, the fine art galleries, the auction houses, consult a doctor in Harley Street or a consultant, consult distinguished lawyers and see a variety of commercial and professional people. The role of the bespoke tailor in Savile Row is integrated into these activities.

If, by changing the Use Class Order, the Savile Row tailoring community is forced away from the centre of London, that departure will damage the centre of London and the commercial activity of the City of Westminster. The City of Westminster Chamber of Commerce and Industry, which is currently looking at this issue, is deeply concerned about this prospect. We cannot look upon these planning orders purely as matters to do with planning and the environment. We have to take into account the knock-on effect of change, and the effect of that change on the character of the commercial community, and in turn on those who work in it.'

The tailors failed to get the proposed business class changed. Responding to Mr Wheeler, the Government took refuge behind the established principle that planning should not be concerned with property values or rents. As the Parliamentary Under-Secretary of State for the Environment, Mr Richard Tracey, said:

'Of course, the way in which planning powers are exercised has sometimes had that effect of influencing economic factors such as rental values. One example is the effect of the policies contained in the City of Westminster district plan. That plan aims to stem the loss of existing industrial floorspace, in particular by maintaining certain specialised trade activities where these have links with central London. The protection of specific uses — by adopting policies with incorporate a presumption against allowing office development displacing specialised trades — has clearly benefited the west end tailoring industry. It has served to divert pressure for other forms of commercial development away from Savile Row and, as a result, rental values have remained relatively low. The federation suggests that rents paid on industrial premises in central London are a quarter of those paid for offices.

Turning to the new business class itself, the Minister continued:

'Will this lead to the quadrupling of rents which the federation fears? My Right Hon. Friend the Secretary of State and I think not. For a start, many of the individual leases held by the tailors limit the use of the premises to manufacturing purposes. It may be anything up to 25 years before the terms of such leases come up for renegotiation. Only then will free market rents mean office rents. Even then, will the premises be of the sort which command the premium office rents that have been quoted? Again we think not. Rental levels for office uses in Savile Row currently range from £12 to £20 a square foot, not very much above workroom and showroom rentals. There is evidence of tailors coming into Savile Row being prepared to pay these prices today.'

The tailors produced somewhat different figures to the press, the Savoy Tailors Guild talking of rents of £3.50–6.00 per square foot for light industrial premises, and claimed that many of them were at the tail end of 99-year leases, while back-up workshops in Soho were on short leases and therefore at particular risk of redevelopment (*Estate Times*, 13 February 1987). In spite of these and other criticisms the new business class went into the 1987 UCO as proposed. The fears of the tailors seem to have been realised, for a year after the Order it was reported in the *Estates Times* that the rent on a small gentleman's outfitter in Dean St, Soho, had gone up from £1500 pa to £7000 pa.

THE 1987 ORDER AND CIRCULAR 13/87

There was a delay of nearly a year between the Government publishing its proposals and the new Order coming into effect. Mr Ridley at a London lunch in December 1986 said that an announcement would be made early in the New Year, but that was put back to Easter. This caused some unease in the development industry, unsettled by uncertainty, and was attributed variously to the sensitivity of the proposals and the likelihood of a General Election (which did indeed take place on 11 June 1987). In the meantime the property sector was already beginning to anticipate the changes with moves such as Hillier Parker May and Rowden's decision to merge its industrial and office departments. A commentary in the *Estates Times* criticized the continuing delay thus:

'High-tech property and studio workshops slip the legislative net, and local authority planners are being left to make big decisions — or not — on the basis of little more than rumours of change. By prevaricating in the way it has, the Government is creating uncertainty, and hampering economic growth. And what do the DOE's official spokesmen have to say about all this? The official response is as follows: "Ministers are still considering the issue and have yet to decide on the final contents of the Use Classes Order. Nor have they decided when it will be implemented." This is not what the property industry wants to hear. It's time Nicholas Ridley kept some of his promises.' (*Estates Times*, 27 February 1987)

The uncertainty came to an end when the Town and Country Planning (Use Classes) Order 1987 was made on 28 April, and announced to Parliament by the Secretary of State on 6 May. In his written answer to a Parliamentary Question from Mr John Heddle, MP for Mid Staffordshire, Mr Ridley said this:

'We are grateful to all those who commented on the proposals in our consultation paper last June on the revision of the Order. I have today

published a new Order, which will come into force on 1 June. The Order which extends to England and Wales takes full account of all the views expressed to us. Modernising the Order will reduce the need for planning applications, but retain effective control over changes of use where that is needed because of their environmental consequences or relationship with other uses. The major change in the modernised Order will allow more flexible use of business premises. A new business class will be created...'
(Press notice 209 1987)

The Order reduced the number of classes from the 1972 UCO's 18 to 16, with numerous other changes, and was accompanied by Circular 13/87, which provided guidance and interpretation.

The reaction to the published Order followed predictable lines, with headlines in the professional press like 'A beanfeast on the menu?' and 'Use classes changes set to pay off for developers' (*Estates Times* 15 May 1987). The new business class attracted the most attention, with several major developers (including Great Portland Estates, with extensive holdings north of Oxford Street likely to be affected) expressing satisfaction at the changes. Slough Estates (whose chairman had been on the PAG sub-group) played down the effect on its portfolio, but did recognise that developers with industrial landholdings on the edge of suburban towns (and M25 towns in particular) stood to gain while town centre office markets continue to feel the pinch of tight planning restrictions (*Estates Times* 15 May 1987).

PD CHANGE OF USE BETWEEN USE CLASSES

On the same day that the new UCO came into effect, the GDO provisions for change of use between use classes were changed by the Town and Country Planning General Development (Amendment) (No. 2) Order 1987 (SI 1987 No. 765). This allowed certain changes of use between the A1, A2 and A3 Classes and between the B1, B2 and B8 Classes. PD rights to change from General Industrial and Warehousing to Light Industrial had existed under Class III of previous GDOs, and the new GDO substituted the new classes for the old, thus allowing unrestricted change of use from B2 and B8 into B1. Because of a mistake in the drafting, however, the 235 square metres restriction, which formerly only applied to interchange between Classes III and X, was applied to all changes to B1. Subsequently, when a revised and consolidated GDO was made in 1988 (SI 1988 No. 1813, coming into force on 5 December 1988), the mistake was corrected, and other alterations made. The present change of use provisions read as follows:

Part 3
CHANGES OF USE

Class A. Development consisting of a change of the use of a building to a use falling within Class A1 (shops) of the Schedule to the Use Classes Order from a use falling within Class A3 (food and drink) of that Schedule or from a use for the sale, or display for sale, of motor vehicles

Class B. Development consisting of a change of the use of a building–

(a) to a use for any purpose falling within Class B1 (business) of the Schedule to the Use Classes Order from any use falling within Class B2 (general industrial) or B8 (storage and distribution) of that Schedule;

(b) to a use for any purpose falling within Class B8 (storage and distribution) of that Schedule from any use falling within Class B1 (business) or B2 (general industrial).

B.1 Development is not permitted by Class B where the change is to or from a use falling within Class B8 of that Schedule, if the change of use relates to more than 235 square metres of floorspace in the building.

Class C. Development consisting of a change of use to a use falling within Class A2 (financial and professional services) of the Schedule to the Use Classes Order from a use falling within Class A3 (food and drink) of that Schedule.

Class D. Development consisting of a change of use of any premises with a display window at ground floor level to a use falling within Class A1 (shops) of the Schedule to the Use Classes Order from a use falling within Class A2 (financial and professional services) of that Schedule.

Class E. Development consisting of change in the use of any building or other land from a use permitted by a planning permission granted on an application, to another use which that permission would have specifically authorised when it was granted.

E.1 Development is not permitted by Class E if –

(a) the application for planning permission referred to was made before the date of coming into force of this order;

(b) it would be carried out more than ten years after the grant of planning permission; or

(c) it would result in the breach of any condition, limitation or specification contained in that planning permission in relation to the use in question.'

These changes, especially Classes A and B, can have a dramatic effect.

The combination of wider use classes and new PD rights under the GDO means that a planning unit can move between a variety of uses without coming under planning control. Theoretically it is possible for a factory or warehouse to become a shop without the need for planning permission, through a process of karma, in this way: a warehouse or general industrial use can become light industrial under permitted development rights (GDO 1981); light industrial can now become an office (both are Class B1); an office with services principally to members of the public joins the financial and professional services Class A2 (may or may not require planning permission, following *Rann's* case); Class A2 can become a shop under permitted development rights (proposed change).

The exploitation of the regulations in this way would be quite legitimate, and highlights the particular difficulty of distinguishing a business class use (B1) from a financial and professional services use (A2). It does seem surprising that the UCO should give so much freedom for premises to become shops, at a time when changes in retailing practice are making many small shop units uneconomic, and it might have been more appropriate to give a greater freedom for shop premises to change to another use.

The 1988 GDO also clarified the position on flexible planning permissions. Planning permissions are sometimes worded in the alternative (Use X or Use Y), and the law has been unclear whether, once Use X has been implemented, a planning permission is required to change to Use Y. ... The point may be significant when considering the effect of a permission to either Class A2 or B1 office development.

Chapter 3

The A classes

The 1987 UCO is the first to group together three classes (A1, A2 and A3) which 'will generally be found in shopping areas'. PAG's most complex proposals related to these uses, with four possible successive stages of reform suggested, leaving it for policy-makers to decide how far down the path they wished to go. The Government did not support many of PAG's more radical recommendations in this area because of the strength of representations (particularly on merging retail and non-retail uses in one class) and the complex planning issues which shopping areas raise (King 1987, Kirby and Holf 1986). The RICS, for instance, was particularly concerned about the effects on shop frontages:

'Many outlets providing services prefer high street locations so as to benefit from the pedestrian flow generated by the purely retail outlets in the area. Although it is therefore unlikely that if left to the market a string of outlets providing services only would arise, the need to maintain the continuity of retail shopping frontages is vital if the liveliness of shopping areas is to be maintained, It is for this reason that we would only support proposed stage 4 if it expressly excluded ground floor shop premises and was thereby confined to upper floors.' (RICS 1986a)

Circular 13/87 explained the new classes in Part A thus:

'The character and vitality of shopping centres depend on many factors such as size, location, access, number and range of shops and other facilities, and thus on the number of people who can be attracted. Service uses, including fast food restaurants, contribute to that vitality. In addition, fast food restaurants often help to create employment opportunities, particularly for young people.

16. The separate use classes will enable the local planning authority to influence the broad composition of shopping areas in terms of land-use; they should not be used in the absence of good planning to keep particular uses out of shopping areas.'

CLASS A1. SHOPS

Use for all or any of the following purposes–

(a) for the retail sale of goods other than hot food,
This exclusion existed in the 1972 UCO.

(b) as a post office,
This was included in the 1972 UCO definition of shop.

(c) for the sale of tickets or as a travel agency,
This was included in the 1972 UCO definition of shop.

Intriguingly, a travel agency is not considered to constitute a shop for the offence of Sunday trading within the meaning of sections 47 and 74 of the Shops Act 1950. In the case of *Erewash Borough Council* v. *Ilkeston Consumer Co-operative Society Ltd* (reported in *The Independent*, 30 June 1988), the travel agent's business of booking hotel accommodation and issuing travel tickets was in no way comparable with or analogous to the typical retail shopkeeper's activity of selling goods across the counter or off the supermarket shelf. The judge in that case found that it was not the holidays or the hotel accommodation but advice about the booking of those things for which the public came to the premises.

**(d) for the sale of sandwiches or other cold food for consumption
       off the premises,**
The 1972 UCO definition of 'shop' excluded 'restaurant, snackbar or cafe', but previous UCOs had not mentioned them. To clarify the position in relation to the new food and drink class (A3), circular 13/87 states:

> 'in considering where individual uses fall it is the primary purpose that should be considered; a sandwich bar does not cease to be in the shops class merely because it also sells hot drinks, or if a few customers eat on the premises':

This distinction may be rather harder to draw in practice than in theory, and one can envisage future appeals against enforcement which use ground (b) in this connection. The RTPI also identified a problem with 'sandwich shops':

> 'where prepared sandwiches and other foods are taken away from a bakers or grocers. In the winter, such premises tend to expand their sales of hot foods. Problems could arise if there is pressure from owners for their use to be classified as prepared food when this might be just an ancillary use.'

(e) for hairdressing,
This was included in the 1972 UCO definition of shop.

(f) for the direction of funerals,

'Undertaker' was included in the 1972 UCO definition of shop. The RTPI tried unsuccessfully to get this excluded from the shop class, arguing that:

> 'Problems of amenity have arisen where an existing shop close to dwellings (perhaps next door in a terrace) has changed to an undertaker's premises without the need for permission. Undertaker's premises involve rooms for embalming and laying out of the deceased, vehicle garaging, vehicle movements and other activities on a 24 hour basis. Many residents have expressed concern at these activities when they take place close to their homes.'

It recommended that this use could be better included in the non-residential institutions class, but the 1987 UCO has kept the existing situation. The storage of bodies has been held to be incidental to such a use (James 1973, p.26).

(g) for the display of goods for sale,

This is a new category in the 1987 UCO; motor vehicle sales are excluded (see Article 3(6)). The RTPI commented that:

> 'The term "showroom" does not distinguish between "retail" and "trade" premises. Concern has been expressed that the proposal if not carefully drafted could allow some existing warehouse accommodation to be utilised for retail purposes to the detriment of existing retail centres.'

(h) for the hiring out of domestic or personal goods or articles,

This was a new use introduced in the 1987 UCO, and presumably includes plant and DIY equipment hire.

(i) for the reception of goods to be washed, cleaned or repaired,

This was included in the 1972 UCO definition of shop. Launderettes are, however, excluded by Article 3(6).

where the sale, display or services is to visiting members of the public

This is a new wording introduced by the 1987 UCO. Previous UCOs had used the phrase 'or for any other purpose appropriate to a shopping area', which the PAG report thought created 'vagueness and uncertainty' and which do not exist in the corresponding UCO in force in Scotland. The new phrasing of the class has been more careful by expressly including certain additional uses.

Generally the shops class has now been improved and clarified, removing some anomalies in previous UCOs. There seem, in practice, to have been few problems arising from those anomalies, so the 1987 UCO changes should be regarded as a rationalisation, with minimal effect on planning control. The GPM considered drawing a distinction between shops for the sale of goods and shops from which services are provided (para. 14):

'However that would mean removing from the shops class several uses that the public expect to find in primary shopping areas — hairdressers, travel and ticket agencies, funeral directors, post offices and premises for the reception of goods to be washed, cleaned or repaired. The Government has concluded that it would be best to retain these in the shops class and also to add to that class use as a showroom (except as a motor vehicle showroom), and use by businesses for the hiring out of domestic or personal goods or articles.'

'Tripe shop', 'shop for the sale of pet animals or birds' and 'cats-meat shop' had been excluded from the shop definition in previous UCOs, but these exclusions are no longer considered necessary, 'bearing in mind the conditions under which the trades in question are now obliged to operate' (PAG 1985, para. 6.05), presumably a reference to environmental health powers.

Although retail warehouses are not specifically mentioned anywhere in the 1987 UCO, circular 13/87 (para. 23) makes it clear 'that retail warehouses — where the main purpose is the sale of goods direct to visiting members of the public — will generally fall within the shops class however much floor space is used for storage'. Also one would expect garden centres (not mentioned in the 1987 UCO or the circular, but the subject of concern by the RPTI) to fall within Class A1.

Formerly an open space used for retail sales was not to be regarded as falling within the shop use class, following the case of *Smith* v. *Watts* (1963), but presumably that no longer applies, since the new Article 3(1) makes it clear that a use class relates to land or buildings.

The question whether some additional use can be regarded as ordinarily incidental to retail trade generally was addressed in the case of *Hussain* v. *SSE* (1971). This concerned a corner shop which kept and slaughtered chickens on the premises in accordance with Muslim ritual, thereby attracting an enforcement notice. It was held, dismissing the appeal, that in deciding whether a use was ordinarily incidental to the keeping and running of a retail shop one had to inquire whether it was ordinarily incidental to retail trade generally; that in doing so one had not to consider the requirements of particular localities, areas and customers (the shop was in a largely Muslim neighbourhood) but to look at the shop as an activity as a whole.

CLASS A2. FINANCIAL AND PROFESSIONAL SERVICES

Use for the provision of –
(a) financial services, or
(b) professional services (other than health or medical services), or
(c) any other services (including use as a betting office) which it is appropriate to provide in a shopping area, where the services are provided principally to visiting members of the public.

This is a reorganisation of Class II of the 1972 UCO, encompassing certain types of office already included in the 1972 definition ('bank and premises occupied by an estate agency, building society, or employment agency), and bringing in betting offices (formally excluded from the definition). Two other uses had been excluded from the definition of 'office' in the 1972 UCO: post offices, which fall within the shops class (A1), and '(for office purposes only) for the business of car hire and driving instruction', which are now in part *sui generis* uses under Article 3(6).

The new Class A2 is one of the major changes introduced by the 1987 UCO, not least because of its relationship with the new business class, and may pose major problems of interpretation, so it is worth examining in some detail the justification for it. The PAG report had considered merging all uses appropriate to a shopping area, and said this on the subject:

'6.09 There are ... certain types of use which are commonly found in or near shopping streets which entail the provision of services to the public who visit the premises for the purpose. Examples are the professional services offered by lawyers, accountants, surveyors, doctors and dentists. There are also similar commercial services offered for example by mortgage brokers, insurance brokers specialising in domestic and motor insurance, and the services offered by voluntary organisations such as citizens advice bureaux and law centres.

6.10. Under the existing law, most of these uses are held to be office uses falling within Class II of the UCO, and in consequence planning permission is likely to be needed to begin one of these activities in premises hitherto used for Class I purposes. There is no doubt about current pressures in some areas to transfer premises having Class I use rights to uses of the type described in para. 6.09. We have therefore considered the controversial proposition that the boundaries between Class I ... and Class II should be redrawn so that all uses of premises to provide goods *and services* of a retail nature to the public visiting the premises for the purpose (excluding existing Class X uses) would be included within Class I.

6.11. There are arguments which can be made for and against this proposal:

For

(1) The boundary between retailing goods and retailing services is
     artificial ... In particular, a large number of organisations and
     professions which were largely distinct in the services which they
     offered 40 years ago have now diversified into each other's traditional
     markets, and under the pressure of competition this trend is likely to
     continue. This is particularly so in the provision of financial services:
     banks are offering an increasing range of such services, relating both
     to real and financial property including securities; building societies
     are moving, within the relevant statutes, into traditional clearing
     bank business and perhaps into property transfer.

(2) Greater freedom of location of such activities, particularly in
     shopping areas, would be to the advantage of the public: the
     transaction of financial business goes hand in hand with the retailing
     of goods both for buyer and seller. It is convenient to combine
     shopping trips with the conduct of domestic business involving
     professional and other services.

(3) The provision of such services does not necessarily imply a drastic
     change in the appearance of shopping areas. Such changes would
     often be subject to specific control and in any case increasingly it is
     commercially advantageous for such activities to be conducted from a
     frontage which looks like that of a shop rather than of an office as
     traditionally conceived.

(4) There are insufficient grounds for interfering to prevent the market
     from determining the use of premises as between the sale of goods
     and the provision of retail services. Planning should not be used to
     protect activities from commercial competition unless there are
     countervailing public reasons for doing so. Freedom of adaptation is
     likely to strengthen the ability of traditional shopping centres to resist
     the effect of pressures resulting from separate changes in patterns of
     shopping for goods; and insofar as existing uses are squeezed out of
     shop premises as a result of the proposed change, they are likely, if
     there is a genuine need for them, to relocate in cheaper property near
     at hand. In the absence of genuine demand for their goods or services,
     sheltering those uses from competing ones by means of the planning
     system is not likely in the longer run to preserve them in their
     existing locations. Finally, insofar as an office does not entail the
     provision of services directly to the visiting public, it is unlikely to
     locate in existing Class I premises because it will be cheaper and
     more convenient for those uses to locate elsewhere. This can be seen
     in the tendency of banks to move some office operations to the first
     floor (even where some public access is needed) or, where
     information technology permits, to locations at a distance from the
     counter. The premises at issue are usually only suitable for very small
     scale operations.

(5) Uses of the type in mind present no environmental problems in conventional high street locations or conservation areas; in particular, the traffic generation effects are neutral or, insofar as services give rise to less loading and unloading, smaller.

Against

(a) The special class of office users who deliver personal services to individual members of the public could not be satisfactorily defined. Most commercial and professional firms and organisations would be able to bring at least some part of their activities within any legal definition so that the widening of Class I in this direction would be tantamount to a complete merger with Class II.

(b) The extension of Class I to any group of office users would build up an extreme demand for ground floor shop properties in certain locations which would drive up freehold and letting values, and inevitably cause some shops to disappear. One such example would be the West End of London, where shops are maintained by the planning authorities against fierce competition from offices, in order to provide a special amenity and service to visitors and tourists, in addition to members of the public living and working in the vicinity. A similar process might also take place in shopping areas of local rather than national importance, where local professional firms and businesses are already thriving on the first floor of shop premises, and would express keen interest in expanding downwards.

(c) The inclusion of a wide range of office uses on the ground floors of shopping streets does have a marked effect on the liveliness and visual amenity of the areas concerned, which is not in the best interests of the latter and which the public generally oppose.'

The PAG sub-group was divided on whether to propose a merged class, with one member (Derek Wood) considering that it was 'impractical and in any event would take reform too far' (para. 6.12), and the GPM agreed with him on the need to keep two separate use classes, following the mass of representations on the subject and lively correspondence in the professional press. On Class A2 the GPM said (para. 15):

'The Government sees no need to distinguish between different professional services, as is provided for in some of the sub-group's recommendations. The new financial and professional services use class should in the Government's view therefore include all office uses providing a significant level of direct service to the general public. For example, solicitors should be put on the same footing as estate agents and building societies.'

Explaining the new class, circular 13/87, said:

'18. The new financial and professional services class is designed to allow flexibility within a sector which is expanding and diversifying. Banks and building society offices are part of the established shopping street scene. Other newer financial and professional services need to be accommodated in shop type premises. The new class will enable planning control to be maintained over proposals involving the conversion of shops for purposes other than the retail sale of goods while permitting free interchange within a wide range of service uses which the public now expects to find in shopping areas.

'19. Indeed, the separation of the office uses in the financial and professional service class from other office uses not directly serving the public visiting the premises should allow local planning authorities to grant permission more readily; this is because the new Order will not permit a subsequent change to offices with blank facades and not directly serving the public.'

This new class may well give rise to major problems of control and interpretation, relating to the two terms 'appropriate to a shopping area' and 'where the services are provided principally to visiting members of the public'. How does one define the two terms in practice? Which takes precedence over the other? How does one distinguish when a change of use between an office in Class B1 and an office in Class A2 has taken place and whether it is a material change of use? How does one devise policies to regulate these two office uses? The RTPI commented on the difficulty of distinguishing office uses in this class:

'Whilst some solicitors have a high level of public access, others may have very little. Many professional services operate very differently from the financial services included in the category and very few need the street level locations appropriate to the uses visited by large numbers of members of the public.
27. Further, given that the exact definition of the class has yet to be provided, it is assumed that it might include architects, planners, accountants, finance companies and stockbrokers. Taken to its logical conclusion, the only type of office that could be excluded from the class would be an administrative headquarters. It is essential that the class is more clearly defined particularly with regard to the level of direct service to the visiting public and the suitability of the premises for retail use. On balance, the Institute recommends that professional services should be excluded from the proposed new class and remain, as at present, together with other office users.' (RTPI 1986)

These issues have not been resolved since the new Order, and have caused difficulties for LPAs, with many users seeking to clarify their position with change of use applications. It will be exceptionally difficult to distinguish the primary use in a mixed office use of premises, where part is directed at visiting members of the public and part is of a more corporate nature. One could devise tests apportioning floorspace, employees' time spent on the different aspects, or proportion of income/turnover derived, but none of these would be satisfactory, and one might indeed question the point of such an exercise. The existence of the two kinds of office class was recognized by one Inspector on an appeal involving an architectural firm in Reading: he imposed a condition restricting the use to a B1 office only, thus effectively prohibiting visiting members of the public (T/APP/Q0315/A/88/86027/P4, reported in *Estates Times* 28 October 1988). One LPA (Wyre District, in Lancashire) which continued traditional hostilities towards estate agents by refusing a 'property sales office' (against officers' advice) because of the 'limited attraction to the public in general' found that, not only was the decision reversed on appeal, but costs were awarded against it because of its failure to follow advice in Circular 13/87 (T/APP/U2370/A/8/87866 reported in *Estates Times.*)

CLASS A3. FOOD AND DRINK

Use for the sale of food or drink for consumption on the premises or of hot food for consumption off the premises.
This is a new class, the justification for which is given in circular 13/87 (para. 19):

'The food and drink class groups together a range of uses not included in any class of the 1972 Order — for example hot food shops, restaurants, cafés, snack bars, wine bars and public houses. The new class reflects the breaking down of the traditional boundaries between different types of premises. It will enable the catering trade to adapt to changing trends and demands with greater speed and certainty in premises where the potential environmental nuisances such as smell, traffic and parking have already been accepted. Local planning authorities should continue to treat planning applications for new premises falling within this class on their merits in the light of the general presumption in favour of development. Granting permission subject to conditions designed to alleviate a particular difficulty should always be considered as an alternative to refusal where serious environmental problems are envisaged.'

The RTPI in general supported the new class, although the matter of take-aways gave it some cause for concern:

'It has been suggested to the Institute that 'take away' food shops may produce problems of litter and short stay traffic generation not associated with restaurants. Nevertheless, problems of distinctions between those activities with the extent of takeaway trade varying due to economic factors (such as VAT) have led to some difficulties of definition and this element of the proposal is supported.'

DCPN 11 ('Service uses in shopping areas') addressed the issue of restaurants, cafes and take aways:

15. Proposals to establish a restaurant, café or hot food take away shop will normally require planning permission. The effect of such businesses on the vitality of a shopping area can vary widely, from the 'fast food' restaurant with a buoyant appearance which attracts many shoppers, to the quiet café or neighbourhood fish and chip shop with more basic amenities. Other planning issues raised by such proposals generally include effects on vehicular and pedestrian traffic and the emission of smells and fumes. Hot food take away shops, or restaurants with a significant take away element, are likely also to give rise to noise, disturbance and litter.

16. Traffic issues can be important, particularly with hot food shops. Although some small 'convenience shops' share with hot food shops a tendency to give rise to short-term on-street parking, hot food shops may do this in greater volumes and later into the evening. This type of parking can interfere with the free flow of traffic on primary roads and hot food shops may, therefore, from this point of view, be best located on secondary roads or on sites not fronting directly onto a highway. The provision of dedicated parking spaces may help to solve this problem, but such spaces may not always be attractive for short-term parking.

17. The adverse effects of cooking smells and fumes again depend on location, and they will usually be more acceptable in town and district centres than in local shopping areas containing residential flats or surrounded by residential streets. They can, however, be alleviated by conditions requiring the installation of ventilation and fume extraction equipment.

18. Noise, disturbance and litter are to some extent inter-related and may in some cases contribute to a loss of amenity or character. Potential problems of litter are not, however, likely to be in themselves a sufficient reason for refusal of planning permission. Noise and disturbance tend to become more obtrusive in residential areas as the evening progresses.'

Another contentious aspect of this class is the inclusion of public houses. The Government considered the licensing powers of the magistrates sufficient to control change of use, and noted that 'planning permission for physical works would in any case be likely to be required' (GPM, para. 10).

The RTPI disagreed with this view because of the environmental problem it saw with premises licensed to sell alcohol with the purchase of food:

'Such premises generally are open late into the evening and generate much car-borne trade. Therefore they give rise to justifiable complaints if they are not sited appropriately. Existing public houses quite often give rise to complaints because of a change in the nature of the premises, for example to fun-pubs and discos, even when the use of the site for that purpose has been long established. If changes of use could occur within the use class to public houses, problems would inevitably arise and the local residents would be disadvantaged.

'16. There is no evidence to suggest that licensing magistrates could adequately control problems of loss of amenity, car parking and noise generation. In particular, noise from both within and outside the building is a common source of complaint. In members' experience, complaints by the public about existing public houses, when brought to the magistrates' attention, have not met with the imposition of satisfactory controls. The decision as to whether a site is appropriate to a public house is fundamentally a land use planning decision and it should not be left to magistrates to try to resolve resulting conflicts between residents, other land users and the licensed trade brought about by uncontrolled changes of use. In any event, food preparation and sale is not the most significant part of the trade of most public houses and wine bars. The environmental similarity with restaurant-type use is tenuous and it would therefore be more appropriate for public houses and wine bars to remain *sui generis* uses. It would seem unreasonable to refuse permission on use grounds for internal or external alterations to premises intended to adapt them for public house/wine bar use if the change of use had already taken place. Therefore this is not an effective means of control.' (RTPI 1986)

The evidence since the Order, although less publicised than in B1 cases, suggests that LPAs are resisting changes into this use class, as they formerly resisted take aways and other uses now encompassed by it. The class may prove a major area for imposition of restrictive user conditions. On an appeal in Southwark, for instance, an Inspector justified a condition restricting the use to a 'wine bar/restaurant' because of possible amenity problems (T/APP/A5840/A/86/049890/P2, courtesy of Margaret Linacre). Attempts to remove take aways from the class by condition are likely because of the possible litter problems, although there are other powers of control available. As a Recorder on such a planning appeal in Scotland in 1984 said:

'Powers of law enforcement already exist and it is up to the appropriate authorities to use them, and for local people to make representations to those authorities accordingly. It would be an abuse of planning powers to seek, by withholding planning permission, to restrain legitimate activity for which there is a reasonable demand solely to avoid situations arising from breaches of the law, which breaches are not inevitable' (P/PPA/B/99, reported in *Planning Newspaper* 551, 13 Janaury 1984)

Hours restrictions after 11pm need not be imposed by planning condition because the Late Night Refreshment Houses Act 1969 gives local authorities that power already.

The new class may lead to less emphasis being placed upon shop frontage and more on the total space available, with consequent adjustment in rent and rates.

EFFECTS OF THE A CLASSES

The overall effect of the new classification seems to have been to clarify and tidy things up, setting out which planning permissions are required for which main users. Market forces will continue to determine values in the High Street, with the possible exception of building societies and banks paying over the prevailing Zone A rates to acquire suitable premises for future market share as well as intrinsic site value. Like the scarcity of planning consent for superstores, restrictive planning policies in the High Street have in the past created premium values, but saturation coverage seems now to be moderating demand.

An important issue in the A classes remains the relationship of primary and secondary locations. In prime locations the pure retailer can outnumber and outbid quasi-retail users (apart from banks, building societies, fast food chains, and possibly travel agencies), but secondary locations may experience the expansion of A2 users. A landlord's view, looking to reversionary or rent review value, and capitalisation yields, will normally prefer an A1 retail user, although in a secondary location a good A2 or quasi-retailer may offer a better prospect of maintaining trading vitality (Mackenzie 1988).

The advice on business activity in residential areas in PPG4 can be also applied to A class uses in residential areas and secondary locations. As the guidance note said:

'8 ... It is now generally recognised that the rigid separation of employment and services – especially those that are small scale – from the residential communities they support can be a mistake. The rigid application of zoning policies can have a very damaging effect.

'9. Light industry, offices and many forms of small businesses can generally be accommodated within residential areas without creating unacceptable increases in traffic, noise or other adverse effects. The definitions in the Use Classes Order 1987 reflect this. The fact that an activity is a nonconconforming use is not sufficient reason in itself for refusing planning permission or taking enforcement action.'

The change of use rights conferred in the A classes by the 1988 GDO are unlikely to be as sweeping in their effect as those affecting B1, B2 and B8 uses, but may nevertheless be significant, particularly the right to turn a pub (A3) into a shop (A1). Public house turnover and profitability have always been a secretive area, and traditionally it has been unusual for breweries to part with their licensed premises for development conversion to shops. But now, with increasing predator pressure on breweries as a result of the decreasing amount of beer being drunk, and the trend for breweries to look to exploiting their property assets, one can anticipate more conversions of pubs to shops. The London Boroughs Association was also concerned about the unrestricted change from A3 to A2, which might replace local cafés with estate agents and building societies.

Some LPAs have been interpreting the GDO change of use rights within the A class as implying that other changes of use between the A classes are in principle unacceptable, and have chosen to ignore the references to classes which 'will generally be found in shopping areas' by devising policies aimed to prohibiting A2 and A3 class uses in primary or even secondary locations. In one extreme example, a local plan proposal for the Medway Towns incorporated policies that A2 or A3 uses in retail areas would be assessed against the effects of traffic and/or pedestrian flows, cumulative effect and proportion of non-shopping uses, and amenity effects ('noise, smell or litter'), and would 'normally be refused'. (Medway 1988).

One anomaly of the A class change of the use rights is that a shop is apparently seen as always acceptable, and yet it is generally acknowledged that there is an over-supply of shops premises in this country, many of them too small or poorly located to be economically viable.

Chapter 4

The B classes

The greatest impact of the 1987 UCO has been through the introduction of the business class (B1). This was soon followed (since the first edition of this book) by the revised change of use PD rights within the B group of classes made by the 1988 GDO. Before the 1987 UCO much was heard about the needs of 'high tech' users and the failure of the planning system to acknowledge them; since the Order all the talk is of B1. As one advertisement in the *Estates Times*, Summer 1988 supplement, burbled, 'You too could B1 of our contented clients'. This chapter therefore examines the arguments behind the changes, their effects and the reactions of LPAs to them.

THE BACKGROUND TO CLASS B1 (BUSINESS)

Use for all or any of the following purposes –
  (a) as an office other than in class A2 (financial and professional services),
  (b) for research and development of products or processes, or
  (c) for any industrial process
being a use which can be carried on in any residential area without detriment to the amenity of that area by reason of noise, vibration smell, fumes, smoke, soot, ash, dust or grit.

Changes in the planning system during the first Thatcher government (1979–83) had already paved the way for a more flexible approach to industrial, office and warehouse uses: the 1981 GDO which permitted certain changes of use between these categories, the abolition of industrial development certificates and office development permits, and the decline of regional assistance which favoured new manufacturing development in preference to service activities. The aim of allowing the mixture of uses within buildings to vary according to the changing needs of the occupier, while keeping more LPA control over the original consent, could have been achieved through the alternative mechanism of a 'flexible planning permission' conferred through the GDO, on which proposal the 1986 White Paper said this:

'The most significant measure in the revised Order will provide that where planning permission has been given for two or more alternative uses, one authorised use of premises may be succeeded by any combination of the other alternative uses without further planning permissions. This should be of particular benefit to high-tech firms where manufacturing, offices, research and development, warehousing and other activities may be carried on in a single building and where the mix of uses may need to be constantly changed and adapted to the needs of the business.' (Command 9794 1986, para. 5.10)

Instead of flexible planning permissions, the Government chose to introduce the B1 class to meet the needs of high tech firms.

The original emphasis on the needs of high-tech firms, and the shortcomings of the UCO in meeting them, can be traced to the discussion paper produced by a working party of the RICS in 1984, which said:

'17. The main criticism of the [UCO] classifications is that they are difficult to interpret in the light of present day needs, particularly in relation to offices, light or general industrial use and warehousing. It is particularly deficient in connection with high technology operations because these may involve research, development, manufacturing and office uses within a single curtilage and therefore not fit into any single use class in the present Order.

18. Developers of high technology premises need a degree of flexibility for alternative permitted uses in case the original use is no longer possible, either because of the need to make a change in the mixture of uses or because the original occupant leaves the premises. This need for interchangeability of uses is particularly important where it becomes necessary to change the ratio of office space to research space or production space or storage space.

19. The use of high technology premises for storage, warehousing, office or research purposes may be quite ancillary to the main industrial use of the premises but changes in the mixture of uses (for example increased office space) may at present, if it involves a material change between the principal and ancillary uses of the premises and involves more than one use class, constitute development for which planning permission will be required. However, the impact on the immediate locality of this particular change may be minimal' (RICS 1984a)

The RICS paper rejected the approach of adding a new technology class to the UCO, but recommended two inter-related changes:

'(a)   a new class should be added to those listed in the Schedule of "Use as an industrialised office building for any purpose". An "industrialised office building" would be defined in Article 2(2) as "a building in which the processes carried on or the machinery installed are such as could be carried on or installed in any office location without detriment to the amenity of that area by reason of noise, vibration, smell, fumes, smoke, soot, ash, dust or grit".

(b) It would be permissible without specific permission to change from an office use to an industrialised office use, which would include manufacturing, storage, warehousing and research. We suggest that this should be subject to a proviso that the amount of traffic generated as a result of the change would be compatible with an office location.'

The PAG sub-group report gave some weight to these arguments in its justification for the proposed business class:

'7.02. The object of such a merger would be to allow the owners and users of commercial buildings to decide for themselves what activities or combination of activities could most profitably be carried on in their property from time to time and to enable them to adapt quickly to the changing demands of commerce, without having to go to the local planning authority, or, on appeal, to the Secretary of State. It is often pointed out by critics of the present system that there are many unimaginative local authorities who desperately cling to the hope that, by adopting a restrictive approach to changes of use between different use classes, for example between light industry and warehousing, or warehousing and offices, they will be able to encourage some type of commercial activity into their area at the expense of some other. This is a formidable criticism. It strikes a chord with the experience of members of the Property Advisory Group, and we have given it the most careful consideration.

7.03. A further aspect of this problem is the development of new commercial uses which do not fit neatly into any use class. We refer in particular to so-called "high-technology uses". We have not found it necessary to define precisely high technology, for reasons which will become apparent, and believe it to be dangerous, if not impossible, to attempt to do so...One special characteristic of these uses is that they often involve the shifting of balance of activity between office, light industrial and storage use which causes confusion and difficulty when seen against the present structure and division of Classes II, III and IX... Generally, the organisations which carry on these various uses like to have distinctive and well designed buildings of a specification which enables interchange of use of any particular part of the building, with attractive landscaping and good parking facilities. They are in direct competition for space with many traditional office users and some light industrial users, and local authorities in many areas seek in different ways to arbitrate between the competitors.'

The final version of the business class in the 1987 UCO was explained by circular 13/87, still emphasising the high-tech aspect:

'20. The new business class brings many of the uses described in the offices and light industry classes of the 1972 Order together into a single class with other uses which are broadly similar in their environmental impact. Provided that the limitation specified in the class is satisfied, this class will also include other laboratories and studios and "high-tech" uses spanning offices, light industrial and research and development (for example, the manufacture of computer hardware and software, computer research and development, provision of consultancy services and after-sales services, as well as micro-engineering, biotechnology and pharmaceutical research, development and manufacture, in either offices of light industrial premises, whichever are more suitable).'

Subsequently the 1988 Planning Policy Guidance Note on industrial and commercial development and small firms (PPG4) reinforced the B1 point:

'8... It is now generally recognised that the rigid separation of employment and services – especially those that are small scale – from the residential communities they support can be a mistake. The rigid application of zoning policies can have a very damaging effect.

'9. Light industry, offices and many forms of small businesses can generally be accommodated within residential areas without creating unacceptable increases in traffic, noise or other adverse effects. The definitions in the Use Classes Order 1987 reflect this. The fact that an activity is a nonconforming use is not sufficient reason in itself for refusing planning permission or taking enforcement action.'

EFFECTS OF B1 IN 'ROSE-LAND'

The impact of B1 has been quickly seen in the area known in planning jargon as ROSE (the rest of the South-East region outside Greater London). (In less prosperous parts of the country the distinctions between office, industrial and warehousing developments have perhaps been less important and LPA attitudes less of an obstacle to the property sector, while the special circumstances of inner London are discussed in the next section.) Greater opportunities now exist for mixed use and business accommodation, with business parks springing up and B1 replacing 'high tech' as a fashionable phrase in the property business. As a Slough Estates executive said:

'It's not a question of light industrial accommodation being transformed overnight into office parks; what it means is that we are now able to put the appropriate use on the most appropriate site. Formerly, we were trying to shoehorn business use into Class III, now we can create the product to meet the demand' (quoted in *Estates Times* 1987)

Surrey County Council has considered B1 applications sufficiently important to publish a monitoring report (Surrey 1988) covering the first seven months after the 1987 UCO came into effect (1 June 1987 to 1 January 1988). This showed that in only that six month period permission for 338,418 square metres (3,641,377 square feet) of B1 floorspace had been sought in 47 applications. Developers had clearly been waiting for the new Order before making their applications, and some 80% of this proposed floorspace was new development, the balance being for removal of conditions on old consents. The applications were mostly for large schemes (over 30,000 square feet), and were mostly located in the districts closest to London or the M3 (Elmbridge, Reigate and Banstead, Runnymede and Surrey Heath), while in half of the applications the previous use had been general or light industry. The response of the LPAs varied. Some applications were refused as contrary to rural policy or office floorspace controls. Restrictive user conditions were sometimes deployed (notwithstanding the discouragement to such conditions in Circular 13/87) prohibiting office use or confining the use to only one of the possible B1 (a), (b) or (c) uses. In one appeal case, relating to a new 18,000 square feet industrial building in Godalming (Waverley Borough) for 'office and high-technology purposes', the Inspector imposed a condition restricting the use to class B1(c) and B8 uses only, justified by the adverse traffic conditions.

The new B1 class, combined with the change of use PD rights in the 1988 GDO, will make it very difficult for structure plans to maintain separate land allocations or floorspace control levels for offices and industry, although there will inevitably be some delay before alterations to existing structure plans incorporate the changes. In Surrey the examination in public (EIP) into the structure plan alterations preceded the 1987 UCO, but the Secretary of State's proposed modifications referred to it, rejecting the idea of fixed ceilings for industrial and commercial development for each district, while acknowledging the difficulties of the 'market' approach. A new policy (IC2) allows considerable latitude in interpretation, asking that on applications for industrial and commercial development LPAs should have regard to the availability of existing land and premises, labour and housing markets, the needs of local and small firms, and environmental issues. In Berkshire the county council prepared revised employment policies, but the Secretary of State did not incorporate them into the proposed modifications. In the Leicestershire Structure Plan modifications, however, the Secretary of State changed the employment policies so that the level of provision would relate to both industrial and office employment.

At district level some robust attempts have been made to resist the increase in office accommodation that B1 could create. A survey of 25 LPAs in inner London and the Thames Valley, carried out by Hillier Parker and the Central London Polytechnic (Robinson and Purser 1988) showed that two-thirds were opposed to the changes, and interim policies were generally trying to resist them, largely irrespective of the political complexion of the Councils concerned. Among the devices for restricting a proliferation of B1 offices are height restrictions. Reading Borough Council adopted a policy limiting planning permission for business uses in buildings of more than two storeys to the central area, where there is already a strong policy against additional office space.

Another important issue on B1 applications is that of parking and access. Some LPAs treat all B1 proposals as being for offices unless otherwise stated, and apply the higher car parking standards for offices, while sites with good access to the motorway network may be reserved for uses incorporating a significant element of manufacturing and/or ancillary storage uses. Other LPAs may adopt the common-sense approach of splitting the difference between office and industrial parking standards for a B1 case, and in time one can expect new parking standards for B1 floorspace to emerge as experience of the practical needs grows. Inspectors at planning appeals have adopted various approaches. On an appeal in Richmond (dismissed for other reasons) the Inspector was prepared to impose a condition restricting the use to B1(c) only, because there was insufficient parking for the other B1 (a) and (b) uses (T/APP/L5810/A/87/067522/P5, courtesy of Rory Joyce). The virtually opposing view, however, was taken on an appeal in Godalming, where the Inspector restricted the use to B1 (a) and (b), arguing that the vehicular access was too poor to allow an industrial use which would generate regular and frequent visits by larger goods vehicles (T/APP/R3650/A/86/056453/P5, courtesy of Rory Joyce). Yet another approach was adopted in a case involving conversion of an industrial building in Slough to offices, where the Inspector tolerated a parking shortfall, arguing as follows:

'I find that there would be a shortfall of some 12 parking spaces. I appreciate the council's concern about the tight dimensions of some spaces and the practicality of using some spaces. However, I accept that within a private car park there should be a greater degree of management control and familiarity within the facilities available to ensure that the spaces are used more intensively than a public car park. I also note that the council has applied its highest standards which, while I appreciate its wish to cater for the most intensive car parking need, should in my opinion be applied more flexibly to this existing, older building where your clients have attempted to provide the maximum number of spaces and where future provision appears impracticable ... I conclude that the shortfall of on-site spaces against the highest standard in this case should not create problems and does not warrant rejecting these proposals for this reason' (T/APP/V0320/A/87/67292)

PAG's approach to the traffic issue was decidedly offhand, hiding behind the omission in the 1972 UCO:

'even the definition of light industry makes no reference whatever to traffic, and we think that it would be impossible to prove that there is as a general rule such a distinction between the amount and type of vehicular traffic created by these various business uses that they should, as a matter of principle, be kept apart.'

The RTPI used the traffic and parking arguments to justify keeping offices and light industry in separate classes:

'34. These activities have inherently different vehicular generation characteristics. Office uses can generate greater demand for car parking than would the same building in light industrial use. Many car parking standards reflect this difference. If changes occur from light industry to office without the need for planning permission, a prudent local planning authority when granting permission for a light industrial building would require parking provision appropriate to an office user. This would be objectionable to a light industrial user who would argue that such a requirement was not necessary. If permission were granted on the basis of industrial car parking standards, a subsequent change to office use would create parking difficulties for the occupiers of the building and those adjacent. Alternatively, a change from office to light industry within a residential area could cause problems because of the size of vehicles servicing the premises. Such vehicles are likely to be larger and to call more frequently than for office uses. Light industrial uses often have incidental open land uses for storage, loading and service which can be visually and environmentally unacceptable at a site on which an office use would be suitable'.

The wording of the residential amenity test in B1 has exercised many minds since the 1987 UCO, and may yet give rise to test cases in the High Court. It has kept the wording of the 1972 UCO on the test of a light industrial process, but now relates it to the use rather than to the process. Circular 13/87 explained the point thus:

'21. The new Order alters the approach to the consideration of whether a use is capable of being carried on within a residential area. In the 1972 Order it was the processes carried on or the machinery installed which had to be such as could be carried on or installed without detriment to the amenity of a residential area. In the new Order all aspects of the use fall to be considered against the criteria of noise, vibration, smell, fumes, smoke, soot, ash, dust or grit. In this context, there will normally be no material change of use requiring planning permission until an intensification or change in the nature of the use is such that the use would no longer satisfy the limitation specified in the class.'

On this matter PAG's view was that:

'Ignoring the question of the physical building itself, we find it difficult to visualise any significant difference in their impact on the environment between the various uses to which we have been referring.' (PAG 1985)

Testing the environmental effects of a particular use in the context of this new class will be particularly difficult for LPAs. It could be argued that this test will necessitate a section 53 determination for every change of use within the class. Indeed this was the view taken by solicitors and surveyors when commenting on the Order:

'In our opinion this test will require that even though the premises in question do not adjoin a residential area, individual consideration will have to be given to each and every user of premises in this class and on the occasion of each change of occupation. We do not think that this was the Government's intention but we do believe that it is the effect of the imposition of the test. The further effect of this test is that any existing office use which cannot meet the test is outside the 1987 Order (unless it falls within Class A2)... If our interpretation is correct and local authorities either choose, or feel that they are bound, to follow the strict interpretation that we have given to the definition of Class B1, then the Government's aim will not have been achieved. We anticipate an upsurge of planning applications and appeals against refusals, enforcement notices and tight conditions. We hope, in view of our conclusion in relation to Class B1, that the Department of the Environment will soon issue a clear statement to the effect that, save perhaps in exceptional cases, all office uses other than those falling within Class A2 can in practice be regarded as falling within Class B1. In the meantime our view, supported by an opinion of leading planning counsel, is that caution is required.' (Titmuss Sainer and Webb 1987)

This may prove to be an alarmist reaction and an overcautious interpretation. Much will hinge on the words in question 'Use for all or any of the following purposes ... being a use which can be carried on within a residential area without detriment ...' Does the word 'being' imply that all these uses fall within the class, or should the test be applied in each case (as Titmuss Sainer and Webb suggest)?

One of the more inventive approaches to the residential amenity test has come from Spelthorne Council (Berkshire), which sought, following the case of *W. T. Lamb Properties Ltd* v. *SSE and Crawley BC*, to test all B1 proposals against the most sensitive residential environment, and thereby to apply a very restrictive floorspace limit.

One complication created by the new B1 class proved to be the method of measuring floorspace. The standard method of measurement had differed between offices and industrial, being net internal for offices and gross internal for industry. A working party set up to revise the RICS/ISVA Code of Measuring Practice was unable to propose a solution, other than to recommend quoting both figures, and provoked some controversy reported with some glee in the property press ('Agents in B1 bust-up', *Estates Times* 16 December 1988).

EFFECTS OF B1 ON THE INNER CITY

The new business class may benefit high-tech developments, but its advantages are much more questionable in inner city areas, on which aspect a great deal of the opposition to the proposal concentrated. The determined but unsuccessful lobbying by the Savoy Tailors Guild, culminating in the adjournment debate in February 1987 (see pp. 27–9), concerned the character and business linkages of the West End. The new class, as the Savoy Tailors feared, seems likely to force out existing light industrial tenants around and between the main office areas in central London, as landlords seek to exploit the new UCO freedoms and thereby maximise their rental levels with office or other high value uses. The impact can be expected in such London areas as north of Oxford Street, Soho, the City fringes (south Shoreditch, Islington, Tower Hamlets, King's Cross, Southwark) and Hammersmith. In areas like Soho and Covent Garden, traditional light industrial uses have already been supplanted by new office uses (many themselves shaken out of the City by the deregulation in 1986), and more pressure can be expected as temporary office consents expire in Mayfair over the next few years. Great Portland Estates, with its huge property holdings in Westminster sees the new class as a major advantage in maximising its rental levels and property values.

The RTPI, in its submissions, was particularly concerned at the implications of the new business class for inner city employment:

'37. The availability of light industrial premises provides for a range of employment opportunities which are absent in office positions. Furthermore, the convenient availability of such premises is essential for servicing the equipment needed by modern offices. There cannot be the slightest doubt that an effect of the proposed change on rental values will be to seriously weaken the employment prospects of many inner city residents and to create servicing problems for the central business district office and retail users. Therefore, if the Government proceeds with the proposal, despite the environmental objections outlined above, the Institute would strongly urge consideration is given to not applying the proposal on a nationwide basis, but limiting it to exclude, perhaps, London or the South East region.' (RTPI 1986)

Geographical variations in applying the UCO did not, however, find favour with the Government.

The Business Class undercuts LPA policies on employment protection, policies with which PAG fundamentally disagreed. The approach of Westminster City Council is particularly interesting, because, while in other respects a radical Conservative authority, it has consistently tried to protect industrial floorspace. In 1987 the City had some 2.8 million square feet of industrial floorspace, mainly in the clothing and printing trades, but even if all this were converted to offices it would only add 3% to its office floorspace stock (Parmiter 1988).

The Council's industrial protection policies in the District Plan had already been the subject of a sustained attack by Great Portland Estates (now set to be one of the main beneficiaries of the new UCO) in the Westminster City Council case (1985), but were supported by the Law Lords:

'the test of what constituted a material consideration in the preparation of local plans or the control of development being, as in the grant or refusal of planning permissions, whether it served a planning purpose which related to the character or use of land, and the industrial policies of the plan, on their true construction, being concerned not with the protection of existing occupiers but with a genuine planning purpose, namely the continuation of industrial use important to the character and functioning of the city, paragraphs 11.22 to 11.26 of the plan should stand.'

The Westminster District plan states (para. 11.23):

'In 1971 about half the industrial floorspace in Westminster was located in the central activities zone. The greater proportion of this floorspace was occupied by firms which had been long established in the area, such as clothing, fur and leather, and paper, printing and publishing. Many of these industries need a central location in order to maintain the services required, but this central location also makes them vulnerable to pressure from other more financially profitable uses. The city council feels that the loss of these supporting industrial activities may threaten the viability of other important central London activities.'

As Lord Scarman said in his judgment:

'A fair interpretation of this part of the plan is that the council was concerned to maintain, as far as possible, the continuation of those industrial purposes "considered important to the diverse character, vitality and functioning of Westminster". Here was, in paragraph 11.26 of the plan, a genuine planning purpose. It could be promoted and perhaps secured by protecting from redevelopment the sites of certain classes of industrial use. Inevitably this would mean that certain existing occupiers would be protected: but this was not the planning purpose of the plan, although it would be one of the consequences.'

Lord Justice Dillon also said:

'It is, however, as well to stress at the outset that this court does not sit as a sort of planning appeal tribunal to review the planning policies of the council on planning grounds according to the court's own preference. Still less does this court sit to decide in a general way whether it is a good thing or a bad thing, to put it colloquially, that existing occupiers of industrial premises should be protected in their premises or that there should be more office buildings outside the Central Activities Zone of the city.'

In the run-up to the 1987 UCO the Savile Row tailors attempted unsuccessfully to defend Westminster's policy, and since the Order the Council has abandoned many of its former policies as unworkable, but it still has devices to deploy. Conservation policies (the Council has over 30 conservation areas and thousands of listed buildings) can limit the scale of alterations permitted, as was successfully applied in the Covent Garden area under the former Greater London Council's action area improvement policies (see Home and Loew 1987). In the alterations to the Westminster District Plan the Council has bowed to the new UCO and lifted the blanket protection to industry, but defined a 'specialist industrial area' to include Soho, the rag-trade area of East Marylebone, and Savile Row, hoping to maintain industry in partnership with developers. In practice the change to office uses since the 1987 UCO and 1988 GDO is proving gradual, slowed down by existing leases and a reluctance to offer industrial tenants financial inducements to leave. Some industrial premises are already occupied as quasi-office or studio users, while others may not be physically suitable for office use without major structural changes or complete redevelopment.

LPAs have sought to defend their industrial floorspace against B1 by various means. A common approach was the use of restrictive conditions limiting permissions by B1(c) (light industrial) only, but in recent appeal decisions Inspectors, relying upon the discouragement in Circular 13/87, have tended not to support these unless in exceptional circumstances. On an appeal in Clerkenwell, EC1, a change of use of 1400 square metres from light industrial to B1 was allowed, the Inspector saying:

'While I consider the council's Local Plan employment objectives to be an interest of acknowledged importance, I am unable to determine or give particular weight to any harm which might be caused to them, in the absence of information on the previous employment provided by the premises and more particularly on the current balance between the supply and demand for industrial floorspace' (APP/V5570/A/88/83794)

At another site in EC1 a change of use to B1 of a 1275 square metres light industrial building under construction was allowed, the Inspector concluding:

'In the area of Clerkenwell around the appeal site the use of the appeal building for the entire range of uses permitted under Class B1 would not have an adverse effect on the creation of new jobs at all' (APP/V5570/A/87/82482)

One exception where a restrictive user condition was imposed on appeal related to a site in Southwark Bridge Road, where the Inspector required the industrial component in a mixed office/industrial scheme (970 square metres industrial, 4,823 square metres of offices) to be protected against unrestricted change of use:

'...uncontrolled changes of use of this floorspace to offices would in my opinion be likely in this area unless a condition is imposed, and in that event the loss of industrial floorspace would be likely to run contrary to the Council's objectives of providing accommodation in the area giving a variety of employment opportunities. Therefore I consider that there are exceptional circumstances in this case...' (T/APP/A5840/A/87/068719/P2, courtesy of Margaret Linacre)

The possibilities of protecting industrial floorspaces have further lessened with the new PD rights in the 1988 GDO: some LPAs had relied upon protection of B2 uses, but that is now difficult to sustain because of the PD right to change from B2 to B1. Tower Hamlets tried to tackle the B1 issue through plot ratios, requiring all proposed B1 developments with a plot ratio greater than 2:1 to be within 400 metres of defined public transport interchanges (its former office policy by another name). Hackney attempted to insist that all new B1 developments must be constructed to a specification capable of use by either office or industrial users (ie floor loading and minimum floor-to-floor ceiling height restrictions).

An alternative mechanism if conditions are difficult to impose has been the use of Section 52 agreements, requiring financial benefits or possibly retention of a proportion of industrial floorspace within a scheme. Existing Section 52 agreements will remain regardless of the new Order. It is possible to submit an application under Section 84 of the Law of Property Act 1925 to remove the covenant, made to the Lands Tribunal, which will need satisfying that the covenant is, for instance, obsolete, of minimal practical benefit or contrary to the public interest. But such applications are unlikely to succeed solely because of changes in the UCO.

One case study of the impact of B1 upon a particular City fringe area (the EC1 postal district, comprising Smithfield, Clerkenwell, Finsbury and Hatton Garden) has been undertaken by Butt (1989). In June 1987 the differential between light industrial and office rentals in the area was dramatic: 4–10 per square feet and 20–25 respectively. The industrial premises suitable for conversion to office use enjoyed a considerable uplift in capital value (as much as three times), resulting in a short-lived but lively market in light industrial freeholds. Butt is worth quoting at length here:

'In June 1987, many thought that the new business class would lead to the widespread incursion of City-style office development in EC1. In fact, this view – while not wholly incorrect – turned out to be simplistic. By placing many industrial, studio and mixed-use properties into the B1 "melting pot", the new regulations have greatly assisted the winning of planning permission in office schemes; but development is still constrained by the small size of existing plots and freehold ownerships. Hence a pattern of piecemeal redevelopment and refurbishment has established itself. This provides small- to medium-sized, self-contained office buildings which often display considerable individual character. Such properties are ideal for the growing breed of small companies and partnerships who prefer to purchase their own headquarters on commercial mortgages rather than rent anonymous tracts of modern office space. Rather than becoming an annex to the City, the area therefore looks set to grow into an existing "office village".

'Strongly allied to this is the effect that the new class is having upon the type of occupiers in the area. Traditional industries had been in decline for many years prior to June 1987, but the industrial space left vacant by their demise had been ardently protected by planning policy. Much of this space therefore came to be occupied by "studio" uses: modern service activities which were able to squeeze, albeit dubiously in many cases, into the Class III definition of light industry – graphic design and photography, for example. With the advent of the 1987 UCO, this space became exposed to a much wider market – the new "business use" market.

'Many office users have now joined studio users as occupants of this building stock, and are displacing those studio users who are unable to cope with the resultant rise in rents. The area is proving especially popular with individualistic creative and media companies, and also with professional partnerships, both of these groups having traditionally favoured City fringe locations (Covent Garden and Holborn, for example). For small partnerships, especially, the opportunity to purchase a freehold headquarters as an asset for an in-house pension fund is particularly attractive'.

The effects of B1 over time will be to destroy much of the character and diversity of inner city areas, which Jane Jacobs (1970) identified as one of their great strengths. To quote Parmiter (1988):

'The external appearance of the parts of the West End – where it still retains what is perhaps a surprising mix of non-office activities in such parts of Soho, Savile Row, Covent Garden and the rag trade area of East Marylebone – will remain largely unaltered, but the local colour and variety may in time be lost forever.

'Light-industrial and craft tenants are likely to be pushed out by rising costs as the central office core expands into the buildings and streets which have traditionally been the preserve of small-scale manufacturers. The rag trade's sweat shops could finally disappear from the West End – and their employment opportunities with them.

'Other central London occupiers may also feel the pinch as there will be a loss of service to business and the residential community in the West End. The existing plethora of small service firms – ranging from picture framers/restorers to office printing services – which occupy cheap accommodation, will be forced out to more peripheral locations. Indeed, as they are lost there could be some relocation among the businesses they serve ... While few people will honestly rue the departure of some industrial uses, particularly the rag trade sweat shops, many will feel a sense of loss as the West End gradually becomes more monochrome.'

B2, B8 AND THE 1988 GDO

The distinctions between B1, B2 and B8 classes have now been largely broken down, because of the freedom to switch between them conferred by the 1988 GDO. The removal of the 235 square metre limit which formerly existed on changes of use from B2 and B8 to B1 will further accelerate the trends discussed above, and has dramatic implications for rental levels on the City fringe, and was immediately acknowledged in the property press (e.g. 'Law opens new door for more offices', *The Times*, 28 November 1988) The surveying firm of Montagu Evans estimated that about 16 million square feet of general industrial space in the boroughs of Camden, Hackney, Islington and Tower Hamlets, mostly unlisted late nineteenth and early twentieth century multi-storey buildings, could now become B1, with internal upgrading. The sheer volume of extra office space thus becoming available, coupled with development taking place in London Docklands, can relieve some of the upward pressure on rents within the Square Mile of the City.

Class B2. General Industrial
Use for the carrying on of an industrial process other than one falling within class B1 above or within classes B3 to B7 below.

This is essentially the same as the class in earlier UCOs (Class IV of the

1972 UCO), but with the distinction from other industrial classes made clear, and removal of the reference to buildings.

Class B8. Storage or Distribution
Use for storage or as a distribution centre

This rewords the old Class X of the 1972 UCO. The 1948 UCO had different classes for 'wholesale warehouse' (X) and 'repository' (XI), but the 1950 UCO merged them into a single class X, and so it has remained until the 1987 UCO. The term 'wholesale', which was used in previous UCOs (and was defined in the 1948 Order), has disappeared. In the case of *Newbury District Council* v. *SSE* (1980) it was held that a repository was not restricted to a building where goods were kept or stored in the course of a trade or business but extended to any place the principal use of which was storage.

The 1987 UCO gives no definition of either storage or distribution, which may raise future problems of interpretation. In the case of *Hooper* v. *Slater* (1978), it was held that storage of caravans on land did not fall within Class X, which was taken to imply 'covered storage', but that distinction can apparently no longer be maintained under the 1987 UCO, with its explicit recognition in Article 3(1) that the use classes relate to buildings or other land. The storage or parking of caravans and other vehicles is a frequent source of enforcement action (Home, Bloomfield and Maclean 1985), and one can anticipate difficulties for future planning control arising from this class. One difficult area may well prove to be heavy goods vehicles depots (Smith 1986).

Circular 13/87 makes a note on the new class:

'23. The storage and distribution class is intended to remain the same as in the current Order, although the class is defined by reference to a use of land rather than the description of a building. This should help to make clear that retail warehouses — where the main purpose is the sale of goods direct to visiting members of the public — will generally fall within the shops class however much floor space is used for storage.'

Warehouses have since 1981 enjoyed PD rights under Class XXVIII of the GDO, similar to the industrial PD rights under Class VII, and this will presumably apply to the new class. There are also PD rights under Class III of the GDO allowing some interchange between warehousing and industrial use classes.

In *LTSS Print and Supply Services Ltd* v. *Hackney London Borough Council* (1976) the meaning of 'warehouse', which was not defined in the 1972 UCO, was considered not to be a matter of law, so that the Secretary of State's interpretation of the meaning could not be challenged unless he 'put some clearly untenable meaning on them'. This follows the judgment in *Calcaria Construction* v. *SSE* (1974), where it was held that an outline planning permission as a warehouse for distributing foodstuffs by retail and wholesale did not cover a supermarket or shopping area primarily intended as a retail outlet.

One might expect a builders' yard now to fall within B8, but the SSE apparently still regards it as a *sui generis* use, albeit not one of the Article 3(6) exclusions.

In a Section 53 determination, the Secretary of State held that:

'A use as a builder's yard is regarded as one that contains a number of elements, including storage of equipment and vehicles and materials, limited manufacturing of items to be used in building construction and possibly an office element since it is essentially the base for a builder's business. It is considered that a use of this nature does not fall within any of the classes of the Use Classes Order and that it could reasonably be described as a *sui generis* use. Although it is accepted that a use which amounted to the storage and distribution of a wide variety of items would be a development akin to one element within a builder's yard use, the view is taken that it would be materially different from the builder's yard use as such. This would be not only because it would involve one element of the established builder's yard use expanding to dominate the whole site but even more because the fact that storage and distribution was the sole use would mean that there would inevitably be a substantial difference in the use of the site as a result of the need for a much greater number of vehicles to call there bringing goods and taking them away.' (APP/G/88/P1235/1, courtesy of Michael Crush)

B3-7 SPECIAL INDUSTRIAL USE CLASSES

These have been kept unchanged from previous UCOs, although the Government has indicated that they will be subject to a separate technical review. The PAG sub-group felt it lacked the specific and technical knowledge to comment on them in any detail, but considered that the general principles underlying the division into classes was valid and should be maintained, while they could be classified into a hierarchy of classes according to the different degree of noise and environmental pollution which they create. As PAG said:

'8.03. However viewed as a whole, these special industrial classes look distinctly out of date; indeed, their genesis seems to date from the offensive industrial uses specified in the Public Health Act 1875. Many of the special industrial uses have fallen into disuse. That, however, is not a reason for removing them from their respective use class. To take any such use out of a use class is a retrograde step, however quaint or recondite the particular use may be. But some up-dating is clearly necessary...' (PAG 1986)

The DOE soon appointed consultants to review the SIUCs. The brief was to establish changes in industry since the classes were first introduced in the 1940s, changes in other planning-related controls (particularly those over environmental pollution), and the frequency of applications and appeals in each class (thought to be very few). It seems likely that a hierarchy of uses will be established according to the degree of environmental pollution, with one way movement allowed through the mechanism of change of use PD under the GDO – the 'escalator concept' referred to in the Government's original brief to PAG. The RTPI felt, however, that specific planning measures were necessary to ensure that suitable sites are made available, and uses not driven out by public outcry: freedom of movement one way from the special classes to B2 would gradually reduce the availability of sites for SIUCs. The RTPIs view was that special classes were useful, since in the rare instances where such a use may be involved the planning system may be the only occasion when there could be a public indication of such a proposal.

Chapter 5

The Rest of the 1987 Order

DEFINITIONS

The UCO has always included definitions of certain uses, and Article 2 of the 1987 Order makes several changes, which can be seen by comparing the 1987 and 1972 UCOs in Appendices A and C. They can be summarised as follows:

(i)   The lengthy definition of 'shop', with its long lists of inclusions and exclusions, is abandoned in favour of a reworded class within the schedule.

(ii)   Definitions of office, post office and betting office are dropped, and transferred to the newly designed professional services class, which represents a clear improvement in ease of use.

(iii)   The definition of launderette is dropped, although it is in substance retained in the new Article 3(6).

(iv)   The definitions of 'industrial building', 'light industrial building', 'general industrial building' and 'special industrial building' are also dropped, partly reflecting the new approach to land and buildings. The definition in the 1987 UCO of 'industrial process', however, is similar to that included within the former definition of an 'industrial building', but with the addition of 'film, video or sound recording' to the articles the making of which are included in an industrial process (along with ship or vessel).

(v)   The definition of motor vehicle is dropped.

(vi)   New definitions included in the 1987 UCO for the first time are 'care' and 'day centre'. The new definition of 'care' reflects changes in care practice, and also case law such as the *Rann* case, in which levels of institutional care were important issues.

(vii)   The definition of 'hazardous substance' was already included in the 1983 UCO.

SUI GENERIS USES: THE ARTICLE 3(6) EXCLUSIONS

From time to time certain uses have been recognised in appeal decisions and in court judgments as falling outside any use class and therefore *sui generis* (see p.6). Examples include a sculptor's studio in the *Tessier* case and a builder's yard in the *Brazil Concrete* case. A new departure in the 1987 UCO is Article 3(6), which tidies up this area by specifying certain uses as falling outside any class. Such an approach had not formerly been attempted in the UCO. If the innovation proves helpful, further additions will presumably follow in future UCOs. The excluded uses are seven at present:

(i) A theatre

This is defined in the Theatres Trust Act 1976 as 'any building or part of a building, constructed wholly or mainly for the public performance of plays'. It was formerly included in Class XVII of the 1972 UCO, and its designation in the 1987 UCO as a *sui generis* use was a late thought by the Government, since neither PAG nor the GPM proposed the change. It acknowledges the special protection afforded to theatres particularly since the creation in 1976 of the Theatres Trust, which has a statutory right of consultation on any planning application relating to land on which there is a theatre. Development plans, notably the City of Westminster District Plan and the Covent Garden Action Area Plan, already recognise the need to protect theatres as tourist attractions and part of the nation's cultural heritage, and contain policies to resist changes of use from theatres. The old Class XVII of the 1972 UCO, however, provided a loophole for theatres to change to other uses without the need for planning permission, a loophole which the 1987 UCO has now closed.

(ii) Amusement arcade or centre, or a funfair

This is now the only recreational activity (other than those involving motorised vehicles or firearms) not to fall within the reformed assembly and leisure class (D2), a situation which exists for historical reasons. The 1972 UCO already excluded 'funfair, amusement arcade, pin-table saloon' from the definition of shop. Before then the 1963 UCO had included use for 'indoor games' in Class XVIII, which gave rise to confusion and was a wording removed in the 1972 UCO (see p.4). The 1987 UCO has added the term 'amusement centre', but without defining it.

A development control policy note was published on amusement centres in 1969 (DCPN 11 1969). That adopted a rather loose approach to their definition: 'however described, whether or not they comprise coffee bars, bingo halls, and other amusements as well as pin tables and gaming machines'. It certainly gave the impression that whoever wrote the policy note was not an habitué of such establishments. The policy note went on to distinguish planning control from permits under the Gaming Acts, an interesting statement which the PAG report and GPM have tended to depart from. The Gaming Acts, as the policy note says:

'do not stipulate the matters which may be taken into account on an application but authorities can for example take account of the social effects of a proposal, the number of amusement places in an area already, and questions of public order. Planning permission on the other hand may be refused or given subject to conditions only for proper planning reasons, i.e. reasons relevant to the development and use of land. The factors which call for consideration on a planning application for an amusement centre are its effects on amenity and the character of its surroundings, and its effect on road safety and traffic flow... The highways effects will depend to some extent on the activities to be carried on. For example, large concentrations of people at the end of bingo sessions held at an amusement centre would have a different effect from the same number of people arriving and departing over a longer period... As regards situation, amusement centres are not acceptable near residential property; nor are they good neighbours for schools, churches, hospitals or hotels.'

Amusement centres in shopping areas have given rise to a growing number of appeals in recent years, usually successful (Lamb and Brand 1983). It is difficult to see why this category should remain a *sui generis* use while the new assembly and leisure class is so widely drawn (and indeed specifically includes bingo halls, not previously referred to in the UCO), while restaurants and public houses (which have similar late and weekend opening hours) enjoy the freedom of the widely drawn food and drink class (A3), and while betting offices are now included within the financial and professional services class (A2). One suspects a lingering moral disapproval of the possibly corrupting influence on the young, a moral disapproval which apparently no longer applies to pubs or betting shops (Wilkinson 1980).

The wording 'amusement arcade or centre' may give rise to confusion because of the PD rights (Part 28 of the 1988 GDO, formerly Class XXIX) which attach to development as 'amusement parks'. Amusement park is defined in the GDO as:

'An enclosed area of open land, or any part of a seaside pier, which is principally used (other than by way of a temporary use) as a funfair or otherwise for the purposes of providing public entertainment by means of mechanical amusements and side-shows.'

(iii) Washing or cleaning of clothes or fabrics in coin operated machines or on premises at which the goods to be cleaned are received direct from the public

This is similar to the definition of 'launderette' in the 1972 UCO, which excluded it from the definition of shop, but the word 'launderette' is not used in the 1987 UCO. PAG considered including this within the new shop class (A1), and the GPM 1986 did not make the distinction clear. The RTPI pointed out the longer hours of operation and noise and vibration problems of launderettes, which presumably is the reason for their classification in Article 3(6).

(iv) Sale of fuel for motor vehicles
Petrol filling stations (and garages) had already been excluded from the
definition of shop in earlier UCOs, and the new definition maintains the
distinction. Development Control Policy Note No. 9 (1969) on petrol filling
stations and motels recognised the particular road safety, amenity and design
considerations of this type of use. Garages are not specifically mentioned in
the 1987 UCO, and the position would seem to be that, if they do not sell
fuel for motor vehicles, they will be classified as a general industrial use (see
the *Tessier* case). The point has some significance, since the repair of motor
vehicles is an activity attracting fairly frequent enforcement notices (Home,
Bloomfield and Maclean 1985).

(v) Sale or display for sale of motor vehicles
The original 1948 UCO did not specifically exclude motor vehicle sales from
the shop class, an exclusion first introduced in the 1960 UCO because of the
possible effects on road traffic and local amenity (see p.4). PAG
recommended putting it back in the shop class:

'The vehicular and pedestrian movement generated by the sale of motor
vehicles from a building is comparable, so far as we can see, with that
generated by many other kinds of shop, and if the market in any shopping
locality will support a shop which sells motor vehicles, we cannot see any
substantial reason for submitting that particular trade to the requirement
of obtaining planning permission. We bear in mind (as we have done
throughout this Report) that any significant alteration to the external
appearance of the building will probably require planning permission
quite independently of any change of use.' (PAG 1985, para. 6.05)

The RTPI, however, argued successfully for this type of use to remain
outside the shop class. The GPM 1986 said:

'The inclusion of motor showrooms in the shops class would have allowed
redundant supermarkets in the High Street to become used for car and
motor cycle sales, and result in special environmental problems of traffic
generation and noise.' (GPM 1986, para.11)

The GPM 1986 made it clear (para. 31) that land used for car auctions (an
activity which often attracts enforcement action) would fall within this
definition, although enjoying the benefit of temporary uses PD under Class
IV of the GDO.

(vi) A taxi business or business for the hire of motor vehicles
The 1972 UCO had included within the definition of offices (Class II)
premises occupied '(for offices purposes only) for the business of car hire or
driving instruction', but they are now apparently excluded because of the

traffic and parking implications. The RTPI recognised the particular environmental problem of round-the-clock traffic and parking, and stressed that:

'This exclusion will need careful definition as operators may claim their vehicles seldom call at their offices; experience indicates otherwise.'

The case of *Toomey Motors Ltd* v. *Basildon District Council* (1982) concerned such a use and the interpretation of restrictive conditions.

Driving schools or offices in connection with driving instruction are not referred to in the 1987 UCO, but presumably are included if they also hire out the vehicles in which instruction is given. Otherwise they could fall within the financial and professional service class (A2), or conceivably in the shop class (A1) or the non-residential institutions class (D1).

(vii) A scrapyard, or a yard for the storage or distribution of minerals or the breaking of motor vehicles.

There is already case law that a scrap yard is not within an industrial class, although the recovery of metal from scrap may be an industrial use. The *Forkhurst* case (1983) concerned an established use for dismantling vehicles and recovering of scrap-metal, and whether a subsequent use for storage of scaffolding was a material change of use. Judge Hodgson said:

'I do not see how an inspector who was properly instructing himself and applying neither a wide nor a restrictive interpretation to the Use Classes Order could reasonably have arrived at the conclusion that the pre-1972 use was not within Class IV. It seems to me clear that, on any ordinary use of language, the activity of smelting or melting aluminium was ordinarily incidental to the use of the land for vehicle breaking and the recovery therefrom of scrap-metal.'

Scrap yards are required to register with the local authority under the provisions of the Scrap Metal Dealers Act 1964. In other cases, such as betting shops, bingo halls and public houses, the SSE is now willing to use licensing provisions under other legislation to control changes of use, but not in this case or that of amusement centres.

Apart from theatres (which are being accorded special protection all the Article 3(6) uses are potential 'bad neighbours', which already require advertisement under Section 26 of the 1971 TCP Act. Article 11 of the consolidated GDO 1988 designated the classes of development to which Section 26 applies. The Government seems to have failed to take the opportunity offered in the 1988 Order to revise and update the Section 26 classes, particularly taking account of the 1987 UCO, since it still follows closely the wording of previous GDOs.

Circular 13/87 (para. 13) takes care to point out that the Article 3(6) exclusion:

'does not mean that such uses should always be regarded as environmentally undesirable and thus liable to be refused permission, but rather that in most places where such uses are proposed, consideration by local planning authorities will be justified. The list of omissions is not exhaustive; many uses do not clearly fall within any class and the courts have held that it is not necessary to go to extreme lengths to identify a class for every use.'

Other uses which have been held to fall outside any use class include: slaughterhouses (also a Section 26 development), riding stables (although they might now fall within the assembly and leisure class), boarding kennels, builders' yard, vehicle storage depot, commercial training college (now presumably in the non-residential institutions class), storage of gas, students hostel (now back in the hotels and hostels class), nurses home (also now back in the hotels and hostels class) (James 1973, p.49).

The effect of Article 3(6) seems to be to establish new 'mini use classes' where its exclusions are not single uses. For example, would change of use from an amusement arcade to an amusement centre be development requiring planning permission? This situation did not apply under previous UCOs, where such exclusions were not identified in this way, and in due course case law may be needed to clarify the interpretation of Article 3(6). A prudent application seeking a change to one of these categories would probably be wise to deploy the precise description of the use in Article 3(6) in his application·

LAND AND BUILDINGS

In the 1987 UCO, as well as the clarification on sub-division of dwellinghouses in Article 4, there was also clarification of another aspect which had concerned the courts: to what extent use class rights related to land rather than buildings and land associated with them. The PAG report had considered the issue at some length:

'13.01. We have noticed that, although the UCO ostensibly relates to "a building or other land", in the main it is concerned with buildings rather than land. Open land is brought within the compass of the UCO in two ways only. First, in Article 2(3) it is stated that:

"References in this order to a building may, except where otherwise provided, include references to land occupied therewith and used for the same purposes."

Thus, where buildings and land are occupied and used together, they are treated for the purposes of the UCO as one. Secondly, it is clear that the Special Industrial Classes (Classes V to IX inclusive) apply to the use of land as well as the use of buildings, or some combination of the two. Otherwise, each of the use classes expressly or implicitly is concerned with the use of buildings.

13.02 We have considered whether the benefits of the UCO could be extended to other types of use of open land, together with any ancillary activities carried out in the buildings occupied therewith. Our conclusion is that the use of open land for the selling of goods by retail should form a new use class. This would include open air markets, the sale of motor vehicles and other similar activities. It will be borne in mind that the range of articles which can be sold from purely open land without the benefit of any buildings at all is limited.

13.03 Further, since all the Special Industrial Uses can be carried out on open land, we think there should be parallel use classes for light industry and general industry. For these purposes the definitions of light industry and general industry should be borrowed from the existing definitions of "light industrial building" and "general industrial building" respectively as set out in the present UCO.' (PAG 1985)

PAG recommended that three new uses classes for open land be created (for 'the sale of any goods by retail', 'light industrial purposes (as at present defined)', and 'general industrial purposes (as at present defined)'. In the GPM the Government did not support these three new classes:

'There does not seem to be any great demand for the introduction of these new classes, and the Government does not accept the need for them. The real problem with use of open land seems to stem from the wording of the Order itself. The light and general industrial classes are expressed in terms of use as "buildings", defined as including "land occupied therewith and used for the same purpose." The special industrial classes, however, apply to the use of "buildings or other land". The answer would seem to be to amend the Order so as to ensure that uses of open land are included in the same class as the use of buildings for the same purpose. Thus, for example, the general industrial class would include the use of land for general industrial purposes.' (GPM 1986, para. 30).

Accordingly Article 3(1) and (2) of the 1987 UCO changed the wording of previous UCOs to establish that the use classes related to a building (and land occupied with the building and used for the same purpose) or to other land. This could represent a potentially significant widening of the Order's effect in some cases.

CLASS C1. HOTELS AND HOSTELS

Use as a hotel, boarding or guest house or as a hostel where, in each case, no significant amount of care is provided

This class is similar to that in the 1972 UCO, but distinguishing the degree of care (now defined in a UCO for the first time). PAG had recommended the radical approach of creating a single class for all residential institutions, considering that they had 'similar or common environmental effects in terms of traffic generation, noise, fumes and other emissions and nuisances'. The GPM, however, while acknowledging the continuous range of uses between the two extremes of a hotel and a nursing home, considered that a line should be drawn 'at a point where a significant degree of care and maintenance is provided to the occupants' (GPM 1986, para. 21).

Hostels have been re-incorporated into the class: the 1948 UCO included them, but they were excluded in the 1950 UCO ('in view of the wide range of uses covered by this term', according to the accompanying circular 94 of 1950). This gave rise to a potential Eighth Schedule loophole (now closed by the 1987 UCO), where compensation could be payable if the LPA refused consent for a change of use from hostel to any other use in the hotels use class, where such a use had existed at the first appointed day.

The definition of a hostel has caused problems, and indeed the RTPI recommended doing away with the term hostel, 'with its Victorian, institutional overtones'. In the case of *Mornford Investments* v. *MHLG* (1970) it was held that a students' hostel fell outside the hotels class, but presumably that is now no longer the case. Hostels often arouse local opposition, as the DCPN on the subject (now cancelled by circular 13/87) recognised:

'Nevertheless, experience has shown that where hostels have been established despite local opposition, natural fears have not been borne out and often the strongest opponents have come to take a lively and helpful interest in the wellbeing of the hostels and their residents.' (DCPN 15 1975, para. 2)

The GPM considered the difficulties of definition:

'Hostels may be of many types, including student accommodation,. YMCA hostels, Salvation Army hostels, and hostels for drug rehabilitation or for ex-offenders. Some of these uses may well be included in existing use classes despite the absence of the word "hostel" in the Order. The Government proposes to make it clear that hostels similar to boarding houses will continue to be in the "hotels" class, while hostels where special care is provided should be in the new "residential institutions" class. There will continue to be other types of hostel, no doubt, not falling into either class; this will be a matter of fact and degree in each case' (GPM 1986, para. 22)

The new class will make it difficult for LPAs to retain hostel accommodation in central areas, as, for instance, Westminster City Council have sought to do, because of the pressure to change to higher value hotel uses. It also creates difficulties for LPAs who have devised planning policies for the opposite purpose, to resist hotels changing to bed-and-breakfast hostels for the unemployed and homeless (Hackney 1985). Presumably bed and breakfast establishments, which have given rise to problems in some inner city areas with high numbers of homeless and jobless needing accommodation, will fall within the new class (see appeal cases reporting in *Planning Newspaper,* no. 606, 22 February 1985, p.4).

The wider use class also brings with it other possible environmental problems. Because of the interpretation of intensification in the *Brooks and Burton* case, and in cases involving numbers of caravans of a caravan site (*Guildford* v. *Fortescue* and others), it will be possible for the numbers of bed spaces to be increased subject only to environmental health controls. The provision of bars for non-residents can be regarded as incidental to the primary use since the case of *Emma Hotels* v. *SSE* (1980). The implications of these freedoms for amenity, parking and public services in some areas may be considerable, and may make LPAs more cautious about granting permission for this class of use in the future.

CLASS C2. RESIDENTIAL INSTITUTIONS

Use for the provision of residential accommodation and care to people in need of care (other than a use within class C3 (dwelling houses)).

Use as a hospital or nursing home.

Use as a residential school, college or training centre.
This combines Classes XII and XIV of the 1972 UCO with minor changes. The *Rann* case (1980) had hinged on the particular nature of the care and maintenance that was necessary for a Class XIV use (see pp.8–9). Circular 13/87 explained the new class thus:

'25...Apart from educational establishments, the characteristic of the uses contained in this class that sets them apart from those in the hotels and dwellinghouses class is, in the case of the former the provision of personal care and treatment, and in the case of the latter that the residents and staff do not form a single household...

26. Unless they are managed or provided by a body constituted by an Act of Parliament or incorporated by Royal Charter, all private and voluntary homes (except residential care homes with three beds or less) have to be registered with the local social services authority or the district health

authority. Registration can be refused on the grounds that the home would not provide adequate services or facilities reasonably required by residents or patients. The registering authorities may consult each other and the family practitioner committee about the provision of health and social services for residents. Therefore, among the land use planning considerations local planning authorities will need to concern themselves mainly with the impact of a proposed institution on amenity and the environment. They should also avoid giving the impression that, if planning permission is granted, registration is likely to follow automatically. It is important that intending developers should discuss their proposals with the registration authority before investing money in them.'

The enlarged scope of the new class also creates new opportunities for the conversion of large institutions standing in their own grounds, such as redundant NHS hospitals in the Green Belt, the disposal of which has been a major planning issue for some time (Montgomery 1986). The emphasis in the circular on the 'care' element may be difficult to apply in the case of the 'residential school, college or training centre' category, and the inclusion of 'training centre' for the first time in a use class creates the opportunity for institutions to be converted into company training centres without consent. The RTPI had expressed concern about this aspect:

'Confusion may also occur with regard to residential accommodation provided at educational institutions. Such accommodation is often separated from teaching accommodation and is increasingly used for tourism. Given the length of teaching terms arguments may occur on which is the ancillary use!' (RTPI 1986).

Some LPAs have informal statutory policies for these kinds of uses. Blackpool's policy, to resist C2 uses from locating in defined 'prime holiday areas' of the town, was designed partly to protect the holiday trade by preserving the best holiday accommodation areas, and partly to direct rest homes for the elderly to suitable areas sheltered from the main impact of the holiday trade. The policy was supported by the Inspector in one appeal postdating the 1987 UCO, when change of use from hotel to C2 use was not allowed (T/APP/Q2310/A/87/079718/P3, cited in Planning Appeals Digest). In another case in Thanet, however, change of use from a dwellinghouse to C2 use was allowed, notwithstanding the LPA's policy to resist the increase in the old persons' homes. The Inspector rejected (as conflicting with Circular 13/87) a condition, proposed by the LPA and accepted by the appellants, to restrict the use to a residential care home and no other use within the C2 Class (T/APP/Z2260/A/87/65406/P4, cited in PAD).

CLASS C3. DWELLINGHOUSES

Use as a dwellinghouse (whether or not as a sole or main residence)

(a) by a single person or by people living together as a family, or
(b) by not more than six residents living together as a single household (including a household where care is provided for residents).

This class was described by the SSE as 'the largest new class' when he announced the 1987 Order, and he also stressed that 'it will help to clarify the circumstances in which the planning system bears on our "care in the community" initiative' (Press Release 1987). Circular 13/87 (para. 27) went on to explain:

'The key element in the use of a dwellinghouse for other than family purposes is the concept of a single household. In the case of small residential care homes or nursing homes, staff and residents will probably not live as a single household and the use will therefore fall into the residential institutions class, regardless of the size of the home. The single household concept will provide more certainty over the planning position of small group homes which play a major role in the Government's community care policy which is aimed at enabling disabled and mentally disordered people to live as normal lives as possible in touch with the community. (In Wales this will have particular significance for the implementation of the 10 year all-Wales mental handicap strategy.) Local planning authorities should include any resident care staff in the calculation of the number of people living together under arrangements for providing care and support within the community, but also other groups of people such as students, not necessarily related to each other, who choose to live on a communal basis as a single household. The use of a dwellinghouse for other forms of 'multiple occupation' will generally remain outside the scope of the Order and local planning authorities will continue to need to assess whether development is involved in each case on a fact and degree basis. However, most sheltered housing developments will fall within this class because they normally comprise a group of individual dwellinghouses.'

The dwellinghouses class is significant as the first time such a class has been included in the UCO, but in its present form is a much enfeebled and truncated version of the original PAG proposal. It omits the element of business activity which PAG had recommended but which provoked considerable controversy and was abandoned (see pp.20–21). PAG had applied the principle of the light industrial class to business activity at home, recommending inclusion in the class of:

'the use of a building by any resident concurrently with his or her occupation of the property for any activity compatible with that principal use, which (1) can be carried on in any residential area without detriment to the amenity of that area by reason of noise, vibration, smell, fumes, smoke, soot, ash, dust or grit; (2) does not generate vehicle traffic of a type or amount which is detrimental to the amenity of the area in which it is conducted, and (3) does not involve the presence on the premises of more than five persons engaged in business (including the proprietors) at any one time.'

This proposal proved altogether too much to swallow, and the Government confined itself instead to a new circular on home working. As stated in Planning Policy Guidance 4, the policy situation is now this:

'Many small businesses are started by people working in their own homes. This will not necessarily require planning permission. Permission is not normally required where the use of part of a dwelling-house for business purposes does not change the overall character of its use as a residence. For example the use by a householder of a room as an office would not normally require permission. It is reasonable that where the business use becomes dominant or intrusive, permission should be required (and may be refused), but many small businesses can be carried on from home without any serious detriment to neighbouring property' (paragraph 17).

The new dwellinghouses class not only omits the business component, but also adopts a lower figure for residents living together than PAG recommended. Instead of the concept of a single household, the PAG had recommended 'use as a residential institution provided that no more than 10 people were permanently housed.' The Government considered the figure of ten too high and replaced it with six. The RTPI thought that too low, commenting:

'Housing associations, particularly those working in inner city areas with concentrations of ethnic minorities, regularly provide homes for family groups of 7, 8 or 9 persons. The impact of such dwellings on neighbours, particularly where there are three generations with several adult children, is no different from group homes of a similar size.'

The emphasis upon the single household leaves houses in multi-occupation outside the scope of both this and the hotels and hostels class, at least where facilities are not shared. The definition of a house in multiple occupation in section 58 of the Housing Act 1969 is a house occupied by persons who do not form a single household. Recent estimates suggest 300,000 premises could be so classified, falling both inside and outside Classes C1, C2 and C3 (Kirby and Sopp 1986).

In an appeal relating to a property at Oldmixon (Woodspring District), the Inspector allowed within class C3(b) the use of a dwellinghouse for residential use by up to six persons for 15–18 month stays (who had previously undergone treatment at the adjoining centre for the treatment of drug addicts) fell within class C3(b) (T/APP/V0130/A/87/077421/P4, cited in PAD).

Possible complications may arise where a dwellinghouse is already subject to restrictive user conditions. The wording 'whether or not as a sole or main residence' clearly includes within the class both permanent residential use and temporary use including holiday use, so it would not now seem necessary to determine whether a change from holiday use to permanent residential use involves a material change of use. Conditions will need to satisfy the rigorous test imposed in the *Carpet Decor* case, i.e. that any exclusion of the UCO or the GDO should be stated in unequivocal terms (Midgley 1987).

The 1988 GDO does not refer to the Dwellinghouse Use Class in its definitions, but merely states that 'dwellinghouse' does not include a building containing one or more flats, or a flat contained within such a building.

CLASS D1. NON-RESIDENTIAL INSTITUTIONS

Any use not including a residential use –
(a) for the provision of any medical or health services except the use of premises attached to the residence of any consultant or practitioner,
(b) as a crèche, day nursery or day centre,
(c) for the provision of education,
(d) for the display of works of art (otherwise than for sale or hire),
(e) as a museum,
(f) as a public library or public reading room,
(g) as a public hall or exhibition hall,
(h) for, or in connexion with, public worship or religious instruction.

This class groups uses formerly contained in classes XIII, XIV and XVI of the 1972 UCO, which PAG considered to have 'certain common environmental effects, to some degree similar but distinguishable from those created by residential institutions'. The first UCO in 1948 had defined these uses more widely than subsequent UCOs in including 'indoor games' (thus creating possible overlap with amusement centres and arcades until removed in the 1972 (UCO) and 'non-residential clubs'. Dispensaries, which had formerly been in Class XV, were not included, because it was felt that dispensing is now usually carried out either by pharmaceutical chemists, who fall within the shops class A1, or within a hospital (Class C2). Crèches and nursery schools and playgroups are also covered by the extensive registration requirements of the Nurseries and Child Minders Acts.

The RTPI argued against some of these mergers. It stated, for instance, that:

'Health centres, clinics and surgeries are often located in residential areas and the introduction of the other uses with their associated problems including different hours of use could prove unacceptable to many residents.'

PAG had noted that non-residential schools and colleges were not included in the old UCO, hence the inclusion of 'the provision of education' in the Order. Circular 13/87 indicated that the class is intended to include day centres, adult training centres and other premises for the provision of non-resident social services as well as non-residential schools and colleges. The RTPI had argued unsuccessfully for them to be left as *sui generis* uses because of their possible traffic and noise problems.

PAG had recommended including places of worship in the assembly and leisure class, but the GPM considered places of worship and church halls to be more akin to public halls. The RTPI argued unsuccessfully that they were sufficiently distinct to remain separate, and that, since the total number of premises in the class were few, any removal of planning control would not result in any significant reduction in numbers of planning applications. Places of worship attract quite frequent enforcement notices because of conflict with residential amenity (Home, Bloomfield and Maclean 1985), which would tend to support the RTPI's view.

CLASS D2. ASSEMBLY AND LEISURE

Use as –
(a) a cinema,
(b) a concert hall,
(c) a bingo hall or casino,
(d) a dance hall,
(e) a swimming bath, skating rink, gymnasium or area for other indoor or outdoor sports or recreations, not involving motorised vehicles or firearms.

This class is based on classes XVII and XVIII of the 1972 UCO, extended to include all indoor and outdoor sports uses not involving motor vehicles or firearms. The construction of associated buildings would still require specific consent.

PAG considered that all the uses in Classes XIII, XVII and XVIII of the 1972 UCO were 'sessional activities involving the assembly of substantial numbers of peoples and vehicles at regular or irregular intervals' (PAG 1985, para, 10.03), and saw little or no distinction between their environmental effects. It therefore recommended their merger and extension 'to cover other indoor and outdoor sports and leisure uses'. The GPM accepted the proposal with the exception of places of worship and church halls, included with non-residential institutions. The RICS had reservations about the proposed class, and advocated classifying outdoor sports separately because of the greater noise element, and urged 'a general caveat regarding noise, covering both indoor and outdoor sports' (RICS 1986b, para 23). The RTPI had recommended that this class of essentially 'bad neighbour' uses also includes public houses, wine bars, social clubs, hotels with entertainment facilities open to the public and amusement arcades. The RTPI also expressed concern about the inclusion of outside leisure uses, which cover a wide range of activities from bowling greens to motorcycle scrambling, hence the restrictions on sports involving motorised vehicles and firearms.

The class does not include theatres, formerly in Class XVII of the 1972 UCO but now one of the *sui generis* uses specified in Article 3(6). Among the activities which presumably fall within this class but are not specifically referred to are:

(i) 'Turkish or other vapour or foam bath' (included in Class XVIII of the 1972 UCO, and presumably still recognised as a form of indoor recreation, usually associated with a swimming bath)

(ii) non-residential clubs (included in Class XXII of the 1948 UCO but removed in the 1972 UCO); it is not immediately clear whether social centres and community centres, which were also included in Class XXII of the 1948 UCO but removed in the 1972 UCO, would fall in this class or in Class D1)

(iii) music halls (included in Class XVII of the 1972 UCO but now virtually extinct)

(iv) zoos and wildlife parks.

Camping and caravan sites presumably fall within the class where they are used for recreation rather than for residential purposes (a distinction which can be difficult to establish in practice). Camping and caravans are a tangled area for planning control, often involving established uses, the interpretation of old and loosely worded consents, PD rights under Class XXIII of the GDO, and overlap with the licensing requirements of the Caravan Sites Act 1960. Some LPAs have attempted to grapple with the issues, particularly in coastal areas (Gwynedd 1980, Humberside 1980, James and Pender 1980), and the DOE proposed but later abandoned unified site licensing for tent and caravan sites alike (Camping 1983), as well as giving guidance on holiday caravans (DCPN 8 1969). The situation is now likely to become even more complicated with the freedoms of the new class.

A further complication arises with amusement centres and arcades. Apart from the exclusion from the class of sport and recreation involving 'motorised vehicles or firearms', Article 3(6) also excludes from any class 'an amusement arcade or centre, or a funfair', but it is hard to see how such activities could be precluded if they were incidental to the primary use.

Amusement parks, however, also enjoy PD rights under Part 28 of the 1988 GDO, added by the 1985 GDO, as follows:

'The carrying on of any of the following operations on land (or on a seaside pier) which is lawfully used as an amusement park:-

(a) the erection of any stalls, booths, other similar buildings or structures, or the installation of any plant or machinery (which expression, in this class, includes structures or erections in the nature of plant or machinery) to be used for or in connection with the provision in the amusement park of entertainment or amusement for the public;

(b) the extension, alteration or replacement of any plant or machinery, building or structure so used; so long as –

(i) no plant or machinery installed, extended, altered or replaced pursuant to this permission exceeds a height of 25 metres above ground level (or, if the land or pier is within 3 kilometres of the perimeter of an aerodrome, 25 metres or the height of the highest existing structure, whichever is the lesser), and

(iii) no other building or structure erected pursuant to this permission exceeds the height of 5 metres above ground level (or, in the case of an extension to a building or structure, 5 metres or the height of the roof of the existing building or of the structure, whichever is the greater),

and so long as no such operation is carried out within 25 metres of the curtilage of a dwelling.'

The 1985 GDO defines an amusement park as:

'an enclosed area of open land, or any part of a seaside pier, which is principally used (other than by way of a temporary use) as a funfair or otherwise for the purposes of providing public entertainment by means of mechanical amusements and side-shows; and, where part only of an enclosed area is commonly so used as a funfair or for such public entertainment, only the part so used shall be regarded as an amusement park.'

The 1987 UCO does not define either the term 'sports and recreation' used in the class or 'assembly and leisure' used in the title, and the activities encompassed by this class seem to be very wide, amounting to one of the more significant reforms in the Order. It confers upon the leisure industry effectively the same freedom from planning control as farming (the agricultural or forestry use of land not involving development of the land by virtue of section 22(2)(e) of the TCP Act 1971).

Of all the use classes in the 1987 UCO the leisure and assembly class has the greatest potential impact upon the countryside and coastal areas. It appears to offer freedom for the owners of extensive facilities such as golf courses or football grounds to turn their sites into whatever recreation uses they think fit (e.g. amusement or theme parks), which may well have an adverse effect upon the amenities of the countryside and Green Belt areas. A farmer who establishes a recreational use on part of his land such as seasonal camping can now enjoy the freedoms of this class from planning control. While the requirement for planning permission for new buildings and operational development in theory provides some control over these uses, in practice permitted development rights already allow roads, toilets, fencing, booths, plant and machinery and other development under Part 28 (development on licenced caravan sites) and the recent Part 5 (cited above). One is left with the impression that the Government has failed to grasp, or is unconcerned about, the full environmental implications of this class, particularly for the countryside.

Chapter 6

Consequences of the 1987 Order

The 1987 UCO is probably the most important reform of town planning legislation to be made by the post-1979 Conservative Government: of wider application than enterprise zones, simplified planning zones or urban development corporations, of far greater benefit to developers and property-owners than the relatively trivial relaxations in the GDO, more restrictive to local planning policies than changes to the development plan and policy framework, and with more impact on the form of development than refinements to conservation controls. It is transforming the operation of planning control by LPAs, which are having to reappraise their policies and priorities. The extent of the impact upon planning control is gradually becoming apparent through appeal decisions, as LPAs' rearguard actions fail to persuade the Inspectorate, although the various imprecisions in the wording of the Order have yet to be tested in any significant High Court challenges on points of law.

EFFECT ON NUMBERS OF PLANNING APPLICATIONS AND REFUSALS

One benefit of the 1987 UCO, as stated in circular 13/87, is to simplify the system by not requiring planning permission for changes of use that generally do not damage amenity. Announcing the Order, Secretary of State Ridley said:

> 'Modernising the Order will reduce the need for planning applications, but retain effective control over changes of use where that is needed because of their environmental consequences or relationship with other uses.' (Press Release 1987)

One would therefore expect a reduction in the number of planning applications. What do the statistics suggest?

The PAG sub-group does not seem to have been informed by any quantitative analysis of planning applications for change of use, nor does there seem to have been any systematic monitoring of development control statistics since the Order came into effect. The DOE's statistics on development control (DC Statistics) are of limited help, because since 1977 all change of use decisions have been grouped together, and because applications for new construction involving a change of use are included with other development under the operational definition. There are 40,000–50,000 change of use decisions (excluding new development) in England each year, about a sixth of all planning decisions. About a quarter are refused, which is significantly higher than the refusal rate of 13–15% for all kinds of application.

Between 1968 and 1976 the statistics on change of use decisions classified them by the proposed use, but not the use to be changed from, which obviously limits their value for assessing the impact of changes resulting from the UCO. Table 1 gives an analysis of the percentage distribution between main types of change of use decisions. The relative proportions did not vary significantly from year to year, with two exceptions. The offices category went up in 1973–5 (the annual average for those years was 21% higher than that for the previous five years), a trend doubtless related to the property boom of the period. Also the amusement/recreation category fell after 1970 (the annual average was 23% higher in 1968–70 than for the three succeeding years), for reasons that are not immediately apparent. Nearly half were not readily classifiable, which shows the wide range of activities embraced by a material change of use under the TCP Acts.

Table 1
Change of use decisions by type of proposed use
All decisions (639,000) in England and Wales 1968–76)
Source: Home 1987a

Proposed use	%
Offices	9.8
Shop	8.2
Caravan sites (residential)	7.0
Storage/warehousing	5.3
Industry	4.4
Car parks	4.2
Amusement/recreation	3.7
Health/social services	2.9
Caravan sites (holiday)	2.1
Betting office	1.7
Car sales	1.6
Education	1.3
Other	47.8
	100.0

These figures suggest that the new UCO will have only a limited effect in reducing the number of applications, because of the great diversity of activities. The main reductions will presumably be in the offices and industry categories because of the new business class, and marginally in the three shopping area classes (e.g. with the merging of betting offices in the financial and professional services class), and perhaps in the assembly and leisure class. Car sales remain a *sui generis* use.

The refusal rate on change of use applications is not only relatively high but has remained fairly constant over the years: in 1968 23.5% of change of use applications were refused, in 1979–80 25%, in 1982–3 22%. Table 2 gives refusal and appeal rates for the main types of proposed use, for the only years when the statistics were published, and also the success rate on such appeals (unfortunately only available for two years). Proposals for holiday caravan sites (which would now apparently fall within the assembly and leisure class) had the highest refusal rate (Column B, higher than any other type of development, whether change of use or operations), and also the greatest propensity to go to appeal (Column D), albeit with least chance of success (Column E). Changes of use to offices show a tendency to go to appeal, and a good success rate, but it is not clear whether the 1987 UCO, splitting offices between two classes as it does, will make much difference to these statistics.

Table 2
Refusals and appeals by type of use change
England and Wales 1968–76
Source: Home 1987a

Use type	A Total no. of refusals (000s)	B Refusals as % of all decisions	C Total no. of appeals (000s)	D Ratio A:C	E % of appeals allowed[1]
All change of use	161.0	25.1	12.0	13:1	32.1
Residential caravans	12.3	27.4	1.3	9:1	23.8
Holiday caravans	6.9	50.4	0.9	7:1	19.6
Car sales	3.8	38.0	0.4	25:1	34.6
Car parks	3.9	14.7	0.4	10:1	21.4
C/use to					
— offices	16.9	26.9	2.0	8:1	40.8
— shop	15.8	30.0	1.1	14:1	30.3
— industry	8.4	30.2	0.6	14:1	29.3

[1] Data only available for 1974–6

In the period immediately after the new Order one should not expect to see much reduction in change of use applications, since owners and occupiers have been seeking to clarify or reposition the planning position on their properties, particularly in the A and B classes, often by the removal of conditions on old consents. It seems likely that the new Order will result in more refusals on change of use applications, because the wider scope of use class rights will make LPAs more reluctant to grant permission, even conditionally. Whether LPAs can defend their position successfully against a subsequent appeal will depend upon the reasoned justification that they can put forward for their policy, preferably in the context of a statutory development plan. Many changes of use with high refusal rates remain within separate use classes and still require permission: changes for use, for instance, to building society office, restaurant, or amusement centre in shopping areas.

Even where a particular change of use is now removed from planning control by the wider use classes, any operational development such as buildings or modifications to buildings would still require permission, unless covered by PD rights under the GDO. This obviously retains some LPA control, but it is not open to the LPA to refuse permission for the building because it does not like the new use, when that change of use is allowed by the UCO. PAG was ambivalent on the point:

'Of course, planning control, particularly over traffic generation and visual impact is always present because of the need to obtain planning permission for new construction, alterations to buildings or other physical development (as opposed to change of use). The continuance of this type of control has been fundamental to the sub-group's consideration of the UCO. In other words, the need for planning permission for operational development can itself act as a brake on the freedom to make changes of use through the medium of the UCO, in appropriate cases.' (PAG 1985, para. 4.07)

But later in the report, discussing the issue of modifications to an existing building, the sub-group took a different line:

'14.03 Again, in the case of an existing building, when a change of use is proposed between uses which actually fall within the same class, it commonly happens that that change cannot be implemented without the carrying out of some building or engineering operations which require permission. Consideration of the application for permission to carry out the works in question should not, as a matter of general good practice, be influenced in any way by the proposed change of use. Local authorities should accept that if the two uses fall within the same class, central government has decided as a matter of policy that that change is normally acceptable in the public interest and should not be obstructed or interfered with.' (PAG 1985)

The GPM and circular 13/87 declined to address the point at all.

USE OF CONDITIONS ON PLANNING CONSENTS

LPAs have always had the right to restrict use class rights by condition, and it was confirmed in the *City of London* case (1972) (see above p. 7). PAG appeared to disapprove of the practice (even though, in the *City of London* case the restrictive condition under challenge had been imposed by the SSE, not the LPA):

'As a matter of general practice, local authorities should not take the opportunity ... to cut down the scope of the UCO as it might apply to the building in question by imposing conditions which would restrict the use of the building to a range of uses narrower than the Use Class within which that use would otherwise fall. The Secretary of State has already given guidance to local authorities discouraging that practice, and we recommend that that guidance should be emphasised and repeated.' (PAG 1985, para. 14.02)

Circular 13/87 was similarly discouraging on the point:

'The Secretaries of State would regard the imposition of such conditions as unreasonable unless there was clear evidence that the uses excluded would have serious adverse effects on the environment or on amenity, not susceptible to other control.'

In view of this strongly worded disapproval, it is worth tracing the history of advice on conditions restricting use class rights. The circular which accompanied the first UCO, 42 of 1948, had this to say on the point:

'Local planning authorities may, therefore, think it advisable to consider carefully the terms of the permissions they give and if, for instance they permit an office of a special character in a residential area, and do not think that the premises in question ought subsequently to be available for office use of all other types, they may wish to take the precaution of imposing suitable conditions. Such conditions would, of course, be taken into consideration by the Central Land Board in assessing development charge. It should, however, be borne in mind that narrowly restricted permissions will create difficulties of valuation for the Board and are, therefore, to be deprecated unless the conditions are really essential for the proper planning of the area in question.'

While the Central Land Board has long since been abolished, the general advice is clear.

A subsequent circular, 5/68 (now cancelled by 1/85), dealt specifically with the use of conditions in planning permissions, and referred to the UCO as follows:

'23. It is occasionally desirable on planning grounds to restrict the use of a building or other land to a single named activity where a change to other activities would not involve development, e.g. because of the provisions of [the UCO]. This may be done by way of a condition ... The words "including any other purpose in Class ... of the Schedule to the [UCO]" are essential, where the permitted use is included in one of the Use Classes.'

This was the circular in force at the time of the *City of London* case in 1972, although the judgment does not seem to refer to it. In that judgment it was held:

'that provided a planning authority had regard to the development plan and to other material considerations and that the conditions imposed were reasonable and fairly and reasonably related to the permitted development it might impose restrictions beyond those laid down specifically in the legislation even if that meant a restriction on a use which did not amount to development, such a power being necessary in order to meet the varied and particular circumstances of the planning of a particular area.'

Circular 1/85 has superseded circular 5/68, and adopts a more deregulatory stance than its predecessors. It dealt with the use classes aspect in some detail:

'31. Even where a condition would not be so unreasonably restrictive as to be *ultra vires*, it may still be so onerous that as a matter of policy it should be avoided. Any condition which would put a severe limitation on the freedom of an owner to dispose of his property, or which would obviously make it difficult to finance the erection of the permitted building by borrowing on mortgage, should be avoided on these grounds ...

66. It is possible to impose conditions to restrict further development which would normally be permitted by a development order, or to restrict changes of use which would not be regarded as development (whether because the change is not a "material" change within the terms of section 22(1) of the Act, or by reason of section 22(2) and the provisions of the Town and Country Planning (Use Classes) Order). Changes of use can be restricted either by prohibiting any change from the use permitted or by precluding specific alternative uses (see Models 33 and 34 and paragraph 70 below). It should be noted, however, that a condition restricting changes of use will not restrict ancillary or incidental activities unless it so specifies; on this see paragaph 71 below.

67. Both development orders and the Use Classes Order, however, are designed to give or confirm a freedom from detailed control which will be acceptable in the great majority of cases. There must therefore always be a general presumption against limiting their application in a particular case,

and it would be contrary to the general principles of control for an authority to prevent such permitted development or other changes of use by the widespread imposition of conditions.

68.   There may, however, occasionally be circumstances where such a condition can be justified – perhaps ... restricting changes of use so as to prevent the use of large retail premises as a food or convenience goods supermarket where such a use might generate an unacceptable level of additional traffic, or so as to limit the storage of hazardous substances in a warehouse.

69.   Because of the general presumptions against such restrictions on permitted development or on changes of use which are not development, it will always be necessary to look carefully at the planning reasons for any restriction, and to ensure that the condition imposed is no more onerous than can be justified (it may be helpful to refer to paragraph 31 above). It would not be right to use a condition restricting uses where an alternative, more specific, condition would achieve the same end ...

70.   It will be preferable if a condition designed to restrict changes of use can be drafted so as to prohibit a change to a particular unacceptable use or uses (provided the list does not become too long), as in Model 34 in Appendix A, rather than in terms which prevent any change of use at all; but in many cases a condition confining the use to the use permitted (Model 33) may be necessary...

71.   Conditions are sometimes imposed restricting ancillary or incidental activities.   Conditions of this kind can be burdensome to some technologically advanced industries where there may be a need for higher than normal levels of ancillary office research or storage uses, or for short-term changes in uses, or the balance of uses, which would not normally be material changes of use involving development. Such conditions should therefore not normally be imposed on permissions for manufacturing or service industry, except where they are designed to preclude or regulate activities giving rise to hazard, noise or offensive emissions. Conditions designed to prevent the dominant use of an industrial building being changed to use as an office are unnecessary, as such a change would involve development of the land and thus would require planning permission in any event.

Model 33.   The premises shall be used for ..... and for no other purpose (including any other purpose in Class ... of the Schedule to the Town and Country Planning (Use Classes) Order 1972, or in any provision equivalent to that Class in any statutory instrument revoking and re-enacting that Order.

34. The premises shall not be used for the sale of food other than confectionery.
To prevent e.g. a retail DIY warehouse from being used as a food supermarket.'

Planning Policy Guidance Note 4 (on industrial and commercial development and small firms) states the current policy as follows:

'16. Save in exceptional circumstances, conditions should not be imposed which restrict future changes of use which, by virtue of the Use Classes Order 1987, would not otherwise constitute development. The Secretaries of State would regard such conditions as unreasonable unless there was clear evidence that the uses excluded would have serious adverse effects on the environment or amenity, not susceptible to other control.'

The imposition of such conditions might still be defended in areas such as industrial improvement areas or conservation areas. As PPG1 states:

'16. The courts have held that the Department's statements of planning policy are material considerations which must be taken into account, where relevant, in decisions on planning applications. The policies must be publicly known. They are normally disseminated by way of Planning Policy Guidance, supplemented by White Papers, Ministerial statements and departmental circulars, etc. Such policy statements cannot make irrelevant any matter which in a particular decision is a material consideration. But where such statements discharge the proper role of a policy in indicating the weight that should be given to relevant considerations, the decision-maker must properly understand them and have regard to them. If he then elects not to follow them, he must give clear reasons for not doing so.'

Restrictive user conditions on existing consents still apply, although LPAs will now have to think carefully before enforcing against breaches of such conditions where the new use is within the same use class. The current position therefore will encourage attempts to remove restrictive conditions by re-application to the LPA. Any LPA wishing to impose such conditions in the future would be wise to reinforce its case with a supporting policy in its statutory development plan, preferably with specific reference to the type of use or the geographical area that is of concern. Some LPAs have attempted Section 52 agreements instead of or as well as conditions.

The evidence of planning decisions since the Order came into effect is that LPAs' attempts to impose restrictive user conditions have not generally been supported by Inspectors on appeal, unless a good case can be made as envisaged in Circular 13/87. In B1 cases restrictive user conditions have rarely been supported on appeal, although some applicants have voluntarily restricted their use class rights by confining their applications to a sub-section of class B1, e.g. B1 (a) or B1 (c), if that suits their circumstances.

One footnote to restrictive user conditions is a condition imposed by a Section 51 order. The LPA already has the statutory right under Section 51 of the 1971 TCP Act to impose conditions on the continuance of a use of land (the same power as applies to discontinuance of a use, or alteration or removal of building or works), if 'expedient in the interests of the proper planning of their area (including the interests of amenity), regard being had to the development plan and to any other material considerations'. Such powers have been used occasionally but not frequently in the past, for instance to discontinue lawful small business activities in urban areas. Such orders, however, carry compensation implications, and, since they require the confirmation of the SSE, a strong case would have to be argued for imposing conditions restricting use class rights in view of the advice in circular 13/87.

CONSEQUENCES FOR PLANNING ENFORCEMENT

The new UCO may reduce the numbers of cases of enforcement action, if it removes commonly enforced-against activities from the scope of planning control. The Government has in any case been urging a more tolerant approach to enforcement action, which 'should be used only where planning reasons clearly warrant it and there is no alternative' (Command 9571 1985, para. 5.25). Unfortunately statistics on enforcement are particularly hard to come by, since the national statistics record only enforcement appeals, not numbers of notices served, and do not distinguish the types of breach enforced against. Table 3 gives an analysis of enforcement appeals reported in *Planning Appeals Monthly*.

These breaches of control cover an enormous range of activities. About two thirds were small businesses with adverse environmental effects, often involving the sale, repair, parking/storage of vehicles (lorries, cars, caravans). We do not know the previous use of the sites in question and therefore do not know whether the enforcement notices would have been nullified by the new classes making the breach 'not development'. The statistics do suggest the wisdom of keeping amusement centres, vehicle sales and scrap dealing as *sui generis* uses, and a case could also be made for places of worship, which seem to attract a surprisingly large number of enforcement notices. Breaches of control more commonly relate to uses of land than of buildings, and clarification in the UCO that use class rights cover land or buildings may create some opportunities for avoidance of planning control.

The 1987 UCO poses particular problems to LPAs in monitoring levels of

Table 3
Commonest categories of enforcement appeals
England 1980–3 (% of 1335 cases analysed)
Source: Home, Bloomfield and Maclean 1985

%	Type of activity
13	Activities involving caravans (including storage, sales and residential)
11	Vehicle repairs
8	Office uses
8	Vehicle storage
5	Farm activities (including retail sales, storage)
5	Vehicle sales
5	Amusement centres
4	Manufacturing
4	Places of worship (usually conflict with residential amenity)
3	Gypsy sites
3	Scrap dealing

Note: There is often overlap between categories.

public access for the purpose of establishing that a use falls within the financial and professional service class. Where the building is already in a shopping area this should cause no problem, but elsewhere it will be difficult. The RTPI recognized the problem that could arise (see p. 40–41), but the Government has offered no guidance on how it should be approached.

Another difficulty arises in determining when an intensification of use has taken place sufficient to remove a use from its use class, as considered in the *Brooks and Burton* case. This particularly applies to the new business class, with its test of acceptability in a residential area. Related assessments based on fact and degree may arise in interpreting whether a use is ordinarily incidental (e.g. an amusement centre or arcade within a leisure and assembly use).

The contribution of additional traffic generation to an assessment of intensification is another problem area for LPAs. The PAG report, while sufficiently taken with the test of a light industrial activity in the earlier UCOs to try and apply it elsewhere, shirked the traffic issue, which both the RTPI and the RICS identified as important in their representations. PAG said this on traffic generation:

'When the first UCO was drawn up in 1948 the amenity effects of traffic were very largely confined to those caused by commercial vehicles. This is no longer the case, and the volume and kind of goods vehicle and private car movement, and the amount of vehicle parking both on- and off-street, to which different uses give rise, is now one of the most significant ways in which the use of land can affect the environment. We would also point out that the amount of traffic which is generated by any particular use is not fully within the control of the occupier of the land or building in question. Occupiers have no jurisdiction over the types and numbers of vehicles despatched to their premises by customers, suppliers or other visitors. We would have found it very helpful to classify different land uses by the amount and type of traffic which they generate. In a rough and ready way, some uses may stand as a proxy for certain types of traffic, and we have exploited this idea as much as we felt we could; but a more detailed and fully reliable classification is not, in our view, attainable.' (PAG 1985, para. 4.06)

It is surprising that PAG should have felt that user classifications by scale and type of traffic generation should not be attainable, and yet the final version of the Order should have included a financial and professional class based upon the equally problematic test of services being 'provided principally to visiting members of the public'.

There is so far little evidence of enforcement action related to the new UCO. Probably LPAs are being cautious in assessing how far their freedom to enforce has been curtailed, and no LPA has yet been brave enough to tackle head on some of the minefields of interpretation.

EFFECT ON DEVELOPMENT PLAN POLICIES

The new Order is making many LPAs review their development plan policies, but there is delay because of the lengthy procedural requirements for approving and altering structure and local plans. The attempt of Berkshire to draft a new employment policy into its structure plan alterations was set aside by the Secretary of State as premature, resulting in an awkward period of interim and informal policies, while the implications and interpretations of the new Order are absorbed. It is clear, however, that there are a variety of responses by LPAs to the new Order, which by no means follow party political lines and range from resigned acceptance to robust opposition.

To take the various class groupings in turn, the new A classes seem to have simplified rather than interfered with planning control, although class A3 seems to have been more broadly defined than LPAs would have wished, and the A1/A2 split remains contentious. In the B classes the combination of the new B1 class and the PD rights under the 1988 GDO have significantly eroded local policies for controlling the growth in office floorspace and for retaining industry, whether in Conservative Thames Valley authorities or in Labour-controlled inner London boroughs. Frictions in the C and D classes are less evident, with the exception of some LPAs' concern about the hotels and hostels merger.

Among the policy changes that LPAs will have to consider are the following:

(i) defining the circumstances in which a change of use from one class to another will normally be permitted, particularly in those A and B Class changes that have not already been made PD under the GDO;

(ii) identifying special areas (e.g. conservation areas, special industrial areas) where restrictive user conditions will be applied. These will have to be strongly justified with 'clear reasons' in view of the presumption against such conditions set out in Circular 13/87;

(iii) revising planning standards for new development, especially parking standards in the B Classes. This could have major implications for the design and costs of new schemes.

(iv) the traditional division in development plan policies between office and industrial floorspace allocations will have to be abandoned, as the B1 Class and the change of use PD rights make such distinctions untenable. So far, however, the Secretary of State (for instance in the Berkshire and Surrey Structure Plan alterations) has been reluctant to follow through the full implications of the 1987 UCD for employment planning.

(v) new policies may be needed towards new buildings and extensions to buildings where these are associated with new use class freedoms, especially in areas of restrictive control such as Green Belts, coastal or countryside protection or conservation areas, and also policies defining when Article 4 directions may be sought to restrict PD rights.

EFFECTS ON OTHER REGULATIONS

The 1987 UCO seems to be departing from a long-established principle that planning and other legislation should be applied separately. If, in the words of DCPN 1, planning control should not 'be used to secure objects for which provision is made in other legislation', the converse should also apply, that other legislation should not be used to secure planning objectives. In the interests of reducing bureaucratic red tape the new UCO has apparently abandoned this principle, although not consistently. PAG, the GPM and circular 13/87 mention several instances where licensing powers are apparently to be used to achieve planning objectives:

(i) public houses are now included in the food and drink class, with the Government 'relying on licensing provisions to control changes of use to public houses' (GPM 1986, para. 10)

(ii) betting offices are included in the financial and professional services class, and are subject to Gaming Acts controls

(iii) the former four exclusions from the shop class (pet shops etc.) are now included 'bearing in mind the conditions under which the

trades in question are now obliged to operate' (PAG 1985, para.
6.05).

Other examples where licensing or registration under non-planning
legislation may be required to consider planning issues are overcrowding in
residential premises (under environmental health powers), heavy goods
vehicle operators (under Transport Act 1982 regulations) (Smith 1986), and
caravan sites (under the licensing provisions of the Caravan Sites Act 1960).
Thus much of the burden of assessing adverse environmental and amenity
effects is passing from the LPA to other authorities, who may not be under
statutory obligation to consult the LPA, a tendency which the RTPI not
surprisingly opposed. LPAs will be placed in the position of a third party
making representations on planning and environmental matters, and will
presumably have to initiate procedures to ensure that they are aware of cases
coming up for consideration. The Government's approach to the UCO and
other local regulations is not, however, consistently applied, since
amusement arcades/centres and scrap yards remain *sui generis* uses requiring
planning permission even though they have licensing regimes under other
legislation.

Apart from its relationship with other legislation, the UCO is linked with
the GDO in increasingly complex ways, so that changes in one require
changes in the other. The issuing of GDO amendments jointly with new
UCOs deals with some of the areas of overlap, but not all.

Apart from its relationship with other legislation, the UCO is linked with
the GDO in increasingly complex ways. The change of use PD rights under
Part 3 of the 1988 GDO have already been discussed. A further complication
relates to PD rights to extend. The 1988 GDO has merged the old Classes
VIII and XXVIII into a new Part 8 (Industrial and Warehouse
Development), as follows:

Class A Permitted development

A. The extension or alteration of an industrial building or a warehouse.

Development not permitted

A.1 Development is not permitted by Class A if–
  (a) the building as extended or altered is to be used for purposes other
       than those of the undertaking concerned;
  (b) the building is to be used for a purpose other than the carrying out
       of an industrial process, or, in the case of a warehouse, other than
       storage or distribution;
  (c) the height of the building as extended or altered would exceed the
       height of the original building;

(d) the cubic content of the original building would be exceeded by
     more than–
     (i) 10%, in respect of development on any article 1(5) land, or
     (ii) 25%, in any other case;
(e) the floorspace of the original building would be exceeded by more
     than–
     (i) 500 square metres in respect of development on any article
     1(5) land, or
     (ii) 1,000 square metres in any other case;
(f) the external appearance of the premises of the undertaking
     concerned would be materially affected;
(g) any part of the development would be carried out within 5 metres
     of any boundary of the curtilage of the premises; or
(h) the development would lead to a reduction in the space available
     for the parking or turning of vehicles.

It is not stated whether these PD rights would apply to the office and R&D
components of B1 (i.e. B1 (a) and (b)), and indeed Part 8 of the 1988 GDO
restricts the application to an 'industrial building' ('a building used for the
carrying on of an industrial process') or a 'warehouse', which can only create
confusion when B1 and B8 buildings are to be extended or altered.

If these PD rights can be taken to apply to any building in the new
business class, then office users would have derived a considerable advantage
from being placed in that class rather than in the financial and professional
services class, which does not enjoy such PD freedoms. The RICS argued 'in
the cause of consistency' that PD rights for extensions should also be applied
to shops and offices subject to 'detailed safeguards in respect of offices and
shops in constrained locations' (RICS 1986b, para. 15), but this seems rather
an ambitious proposal.

There is also scope for confusion in PD rights which might be attached to
the assembly and leisure class under Parts 5 (caravan sites, formerly Class
XXII) and Part 27 (use by members of certain recreational organisations,
formerly Class V) of the GDO. Amusement 'arcades or centres' are among
the Article 3(6) exclusions, yet development at amusement 'parks' has PD
rights under Part 28 of the GDO (formerly Class XXIX).

Yet another area where the UCO weakens planning control is in listed
building control under Part IV of the 1971 TCP Act. Listed building
consents for the alteration or extension of a building are affected by the
compensation provisions of section 171 of the 1971 TCP Act under which
compensation is payable:

'where an application is made for listed building consent for the
application or alteration of a listed building and –
(a) either the works do not constitute development or they do so but the
     development is such that planning permission therefore is granted by
     a development order, and

(b) the secretary of state, either on appeal or on reference of the application to him, refuses such consent or grants it subject to conditions'.

The wider scope of the new 1987 use classes may weaken the LPA's powers in conservation and listed building control, although the Government's consultation paper on planning compensation includes a proposal to abolish section 171. It says:

'As the purpose of listed building control is to enable authorities to impose additional controls over and above planning control where they are needed for the effective preservation of the heritage, it is anomalous that developments which do not require planning permission should, because of the fact, attract compensation if an adverse decision is made on an application for listed building consent.' (Planning Compensation 1986, para. 24).

CONSEQUENCES FOR THE PROPERTY SECTOR

The new UCO will make it more important than before to know within which use class (if any) a particular property or planning unit falls, because of the wider scope for change of use that has been created. This will be particularly important in office uses which are now for the first time split between two use classes. There are at present two possible but clumsy statutory mechanisms for achieving this.

One is through a section 53 application (1971 TCP Act) to determine whether planning permission is required for a proposed development (operational or change of use). If the proposed development were described as 'any change of use within Class ... of the 1987 UCO', then the status of the existing use within that use class would thereby be established. Sometimes confirmation from the LPA can be given by letter as to its interpretation of the existing lawful use of a property, but this does not carry the same weight as a statutory determination (although governed by the doctrine of estoppel). The RICS has suggested (RICS 1984b) that section 53 be amended to make it possible to test whether a use which has already commenced has the benefit of planning permission, although in some cases this could be an invitation to the LPA to initiate enforcement action.

The second statutory mechanism is an established use certificate under section 94 of the TCP Act 1971, which is only available in the limited context of a use of land which has existed since before the beginning of 1964. An established use certificate does not make a use of land lawful, and is not a grant of planning permission, but it does render the specified use immune from enforcement action. The certificate can only be granted for the particular use subsisting on the land at the time of making the application, not for a general use. Thereafter an EUC carries with it the right to use the land for purposes not materially different from the established use, and the right to use the land for other uses falling within the same use class. EUCs were created by the TCP Act 1968, and with the passage of time it has become more difficult and onerous to bring sufficient evidence to prove that a use has existed continuously for more than 20 years. The abolition of EUCs was proposed by the Government in a consultation paper, but was resisted by the RICS, which considered that an EUC was a:

> 'particularly useful device for establishing what is the lawful planning use of land and, as this may have a significant effect on its value, we consider that its retention is essential to the proper operation of the property market. Although the burden of proving that a particular use of land has become established may be onerous (in that such proof requires affidavit evidence) we cannot believe that it is impossible in most cases to provide this evidence from deeds, planning records, rating records, leases, accounts or other such material.' (RICS 1984b)

In an intriguing case, *English Speaking Union of the Commonwealth* v. *City of Westminster* (1973), the LPA had confirmed that a change of use from an established residential club to a hotel did not require permission because they were in the same use class (XI of the 1963 UCO), but shortly afterwards the 1972 UCO made a planning application necessary. In the meantime substantial financial and leasing arrangements with a hotel company had been entered into, and a declaration was successfully obtained that the earlier correspondence constituted a binding determination under Section 53. Such a case involving a material alteration of the relevant use class during the critical period is, of course, rare (Markson 1977).

Although planning legislation is distinct from landlord and tenant legislation, in practice the UCO has commonly been used in the drafting of leases, and the new Order can be expected to have an impact on the preparation and interpretation of leases, especially user clauses. Leases may allow a property to be used for a particular purpose or 'such other use as falls within a particular use class under the UCO then in force or whilst it subsists'. Where there is specific reference to the 1972 UCO then that will still apply, and practitioners should not throw away their old 1972 UCO (it is in any case included in this book as Appendix C).

With the changes of the 1987 UCO the reading of the previous use class into the equivalent new use class is not to be assumed, because this may be substantially different or wider. Leases usually contain a clause which requires reference to legislation in force at the relevant time. Normally such a clause will not operate to require a reference to the 1987 UCO where an expression in a lease clearly arises out of, and can only be interpreted by reference to, the 1972 Order. If a user clause refers to the UCO 'as it subsists for the time being', then its replacement by a substantially different UCO could mean that the premises were no longer capable of being used in accordance with the lease, and a new lease would have to be negotiated between the parties.

Any greater freedom conferred by the 1987 UCO might be a factor to be taken into account on rent review under a lease if the user clause contains a provision that consent to a change of use is not to be unreasonably withheld. The wording of rent review clauses will clearly be important, particularly the assumptions upon which rent reviews will be calculated. Depending upon the wording of the lease, the premises could be valued on the basis of the most profitable use for which landlord's consent could not unreasonably be withheld, but that would not necessarily enable him to include users within the relevant class of the 1987 UCO. A landlord cannot avoid the depressing effect on rent of a restricted user clause, but if the property is being used for wider purposes than the user clause permits and the landlord waives the breach then actual user may be assumed for the review. A landlord or tenant stuck with an unfavourable lease as regards the new Order will be forced to negotiate with the other party. Tenants will have to measure the flexibility of a wider use clause against increased rental costs, or to employ in the lease a detailed description of the use to which the premises can be put, without reference to the UCO. Unfortunately the more detailed the description of user the faster it may become out of date.

As well as its implications for leases the new UCO will have an effect upon valuations. The Savoy Tailors Guild opposed the business class because it believed that rents of their premises would go up four times because of the new business class. With the 1987 UCO effectively making very little distinction under planning control between office and industrial use (given the permitted development right to change from a general industrial to a business class use), a convergence of office and industrial rents is to be expected. The Government made it clear that the market should determine any such adjustments in rental values, and the UCO is therefore working to remove any preferential or protective rental levels for industrial premises. The marked difference in investment yields between office, industrial and high-tech buildings can be expected to narrow considerably, particularly for high specification industrial and office premises in the same location. Rapid rent rises for industrial and high tech buildings may occur, and possible reduced rental growth for some town centre offices. Demand for workshop accommodation may increase because of the potential to secure full office use.

The design of new buildings will also be affected if they have to recognise the wider range of available use conferred by the 1987 UCO. One can anticipate a redesign of parking and servicing standards to incorporate the wider spread of requirements for the new business class in particular, and developers will have to make design decisions about the degree of flexibility they will incorporate to allow for possible future changes in tenant and use. In some locations a purely office environment will be envisaged, but in others the options for light industrial use will be recognised. If the anticipated convergence of office, workshop and light industrial rents occurs, then a new type of general business building will emerge, as has already been seen in some schemes. The option to change between the different Part A classes (shops, financial and professional services, and food and drink) will offer an even greater range of design options to shopping centre developers. More long-term strategic thinking, informed by research and forecasting techniques, will be needed to determine the most adaptable building form to take advantage of market changes within the greater freedom of the new UCO.

Thus the removal through the 1987 UCO of major planning controls about which the development industry has long been complaining will place a new burden on the industry to plan its own future and adapt to market changes without the mediating role of the public sector planning system.

Chapter 7

Use Classes Orders: Scotland, Ireland and elsewhere

For historical and constitutional reasons England and Wales share the same legislation, but Scotland and Northern Ireland have their own, even if the practical differences are small. The government has used Scotland as a testing ground for new legislation (as with the community charge), but in town planning law Scotland tends to follow after rather than to lead developments in England and Wales. The principles and approach are the same, but there are differences in detail. In the case of the UCO, the Scottish Office waited to see the effects of the UCO in England and Wales before introducing its 'Proposals to modernise the Town and Country Planning (Use Classes) (Scotland) Order 1973' in August 1988. That UCO (S.I. 1973 No. 1165) had revoked the previous 1950 Order (as amended), and followed closely the 1972 UCO for England and Wales.

The Scottish proposals avoided the English and Welsh approach of grouping classes into A, B, C and D, broadly corresponding to shopping-related, business, residential and non-residential activities. It was felt that these groupings served no useful purpose, and encouraged the argument that a change of use between classes in the same group was somehow less material than a change between groups (this especially applies to the A group, all identified as uses 'generally' found in shopping areas).

In the Scottish proposals the Government tried (unsuccessfully as it turned out) to revive the idea of merging the A1 and A2 classes (as they were in England and Wales) into a single 'Retailing Financial and Professional Services' class. The 1985 PAG report had canvassed this radical approach, but in Scotland, as in England and Wales, public opposition made it politically unacceptable. One may yet see the issue raised in future revisions of the UCO, since the arguments in favour of the merger are in some respects similar to the justification for the merged B1 class. It is, therefore, worth quoting the Scottish Office's arguments in favour of the merger at some length:

'6. The fact that premises selling some services are already included in the shops class means that the distinction between this class and uses such as estate agents or building societies is already a fine one. It is not easy to see a clear distinction in land use terms between a travel agent and estate agent. The main arguments advanced for retaining a distinction between shops and services selling financial and professional services have been firstly that shops have livelier and more interesting frontages, which contribute to amenity, and secondly that the concentration of shops in particular streets is convenient to customers.

'7.   Judgments about frontages are inevitably largely subjective. In the Government's view the recent growth in many of the sectors selling financial and professional services, and the increasing competition between businesses in these sectors, has caused proprietors to pay increasing attention to the image they project to potential customers. This has led in many cases to refurbishment of premises and to more varied and interesting window displays. The difference between these frontages and shop frontages is much less marked than the difference in appearance between the traditional shop and, for example, the traditional bank. There is therefore less force than there was in this argument for maintaining a distinction.

'8.   The argument for concentrating shops in particular streets and controlling non-shopping uses in these streets has to be considered in the light of current trends in town centres. It is becoming increasingly clear that the range and type of shops and the variety of services and facilities in existing town centres will have to adjust to changing conditions. These include:

  (i) Changes in the structure and organisation of the retailing industry as reflected in the increase in the market share of the larger retailers and the continuing decline in the number of businesses and shop units;

 (ii) Changes in the pattern of shopping with many convenience and bulk comparison goods stores choosing to locate in district and other suburban locations;

(iii) Increases in the level of consumer spending, particularly on non-food/comparison goods and services...

'10.   ... Account must be taken of the benefits which will accrue from the growth of service retailing and the changes in lifestyle and shopping habits as a result of increases in disposable income and the broadening of consumer horizons. Greater freedom of location for banks, building societies, estate agents, solicitors' and accountants' offices, etc., would be to the advantage of the public. It would enable the transaction of financial and domestic business involving professional and other services to be combined with shopping trips. Moreover greater freedom of adaptation is likely to strengthen the ability of traditional shopping streets to adjust to changes in the pattern of shopping.'

This proposal attracted criticism from various sources, including community groups in the West End of Glasgow concerned about loss of local shops, and retail organisations concerned at the possibility of higher rents if they had to compete with financial services. The Scottish Order therefore followed the English and Welsh split between A1 and A2. (One minor variation, however, is that in Scotland launderettes are included in A1 instead of being an Article 3(6) or *sui generis* exclusion.)

The Scottish proposals included a Food and Drink class as in England and Wales. This also attracted criticism, notably from tenement residents of the Glasgow West End, concerned about the unneighbourliness of public houses which could take over existing cafes and snack bars. Planning applications for public houses attract wide public interest, partly because of new neighbourhood notification procedures in Scotland. The Scottish Office decided that the removal of a requirement to obtain planning permission was undesirable, and therefore made public houses a *sui generis* exclusion from any class, in the same way as amusement arcades and taxi offices.

The business and industrial group of classes were introduced in the same form as in England and Wales. The B1 class was felt to allow greater flexibility in the use of industrial land, of which there is a significant over-supply in Scotland. The Storage and Distribution class was a new class in Scotland, and acknowledged the higher level of heavy goods vehicle movements likely to be associated with the use.

The proposal for a new Dwellinghouse class attracted criticism (again from community organisations in the West End of Glasgow) because it was felt that it might weaken controls over multiple occupancy. This was notwithstanding the Government's careful explanation of its approach:

'The introduction of this class should clarify the circumstances in which multiple occupancy requires planning permission; it is not designed to deal with the social and other issues which multiple occupancy raises.'

Residents' groups were unconvinced, and so the class was modified to exclude flats and reduce from six persons to five the threshold at which change of use from a dwellinghouse to multiple occupancy occurs.

The Scottish UCO is included in this book in its entirety as Appendix E.

NORTHERN IRELAND

Northern Irish town and country planning legislation is similar to the English and Welsh version, but with local variations. In March 1989 the Town and Country Planning Service of the Department of the Environment for Northern Ireland produced its consultation paper for modernising the Planning (Use Classes) Order (Northern Ireland) 1973. When the second edition of this book was going to press the final NI UCO was not issued, but the draft version retained several important controls which the mainland

UCOs have abandoned, and thus provides an insight into cultural differences and the sectarian sensitivities of Northern Ireland.

The most significant difference is that the B1 grouping of office, research and development and light industry is not adopted. Instead office uses are contained in two classes, the financial and professional services class (Class 2) and a business class (Class 3), which is defined as 'use as an office other than a use within class 2', while light industry is retained, together with 'research and development of products or processes', in a light industrial class (Class 4). This, of course, represents an increase rather than a reduction in planning control, since two previous classes (office and light industrial) are now split into three. The consultative document justified the difference from mainland practice thus:

'However in Northern Ireland there exists a rather different situation, particularly with regard to the urban centres of Belfast and Londonderry. It is a Government priority to encourage the commercial viability of such centres in NI and it is therefore proposed to introduce a less flexible regime than exists in England and Wales. This is intended to ensure that office uses cannot move to out-of-town industrial areas without having first been granted express planning permission.'

Another significant difference from mainland UCOs is the exclusion of food and drink establishments from the use classes entirely by defining them (using the identical wording of the mainland UCOs) as one of the Article 3(6) exclusions. This goes further than the Scottish UCO, which removed public houses from the class, and the NI UCO furthermore does not include 'the sale of sandwiches or other cold food for consumption off the premises' within the Shops class.

The other differences in the draft NI UCO can be summarised as follows:

(a) it reduces the number of classes from 15 (in the 1972 NI UCO) to 12;
(b) like the Scottish UCO it does not adopt the unnecessary A, B, C and D grouping of classes;
(c) funeral directors are not included in the Shops class, but are an Article 3(6) exclusion;
(d) launderettes, however, are not one of the Article 3(6) exclusions, but are placed in the Shops class;
(e) betting offices are not included in the Financial and professional services class, but are an Article 3(6) exclusion;
(f) hotels are an Article 3(6) exclusion, and therefore do not fall within the 'Guest houses and hostels class';
(g) 'public worship or religious instruction' are discreetly not mentioned at all, being neither included within the Non-residential institutions class (where the mainland UCOs place them), nor identified as an Article 3(6) exclusion;

(h) theatres are included in the Assembly and leisure class.

The Irish equivalent of the UCO is contained in the Third Schedule of the Local Government (Planning and Development) Act 1963, and is included in this book as Appendix F. The Schedule identifies four categories of 'exempted development' (exempted, that is, from the necessity for planning permission): Part I is the equivalent of permitted development under the GDO, Part II is the equivalent of the specified classes under the Advertisement Regulations, Part III defines certain rural categories (including agricultural buildings, camping and caravan sites), and Part IV contains 16 Classes of Use, which follow closely the wording of the 1963 UCO for England and Wales. There is also the equivalent of the change of use PD provisions under the British GDOs, with the interesting inclusion of a change from a public house to a shop. Any disputes on interpretation are referred to the Planning Board, and there has been some case law arising from Part IV (cited in O'Sullivan and Shepherd 1984). In *Cusack and McKenna* v. *Minister for Local Government and Dublin Corporation* (1980), it was held that change of use from a dentist's practice to a solicitor's office would be material, since a dentist's premises lay outside class 2 (offices). The judgment in *Dublin Corporation* v. *Salvatore Raso* (1976), which concerned breach of a condition on opening hours for a fish and chips shop, is worth quoting if only for the judge's verbose views on the meaning of fish and chips:

> 'I think there are very strong grounds for saying that the expression "fish and chip" could and should be interpreted in a common sense way as having a well accepted ordinary meaning and involving fried fish and chips ... In a criminal case however I am prepared to accept for the purpose of this decision without expressly deciding it that the onus of proof on the prosecution leaves it open to some doubt as to whether the phrase "fish and chip" must necessarily or inevitably mean fried fish. What is clear beyond any doubt however in my view is that the word "chip" used certainly in connection with fish and referring to a food can only mean one thing and that is a fried chip or potato.'

THE USE CLASSES ORDER ELSEWHERE

In time the new look UCO may be incorporated with local variations into those countries, mostly former British colonies or dependencies, who have modelled their planning systems on the British. The Republic of Lesotho (Southern Africa), for instance, adopted a full-blown British form of town planning legislation as recently as 1979, and its UCO of the same year followed closely the British version. It did, however, anticipate the new Dwellinghouse class in the 1987 UCO by including in its 16 classes three separate classes for a 'dwelling house', 'flat' and 'apartment' (although without specific definitions). It also merged all the special industrial classes into a single class.

Some of the British-derived UCOs show, not only local differences, but also the similarities in the issues that regulators have faced over the years. Thus an African UCO of 1960 which has come to the author's attention (the country is unidentified but is thought to be Kenya) is interesting because it anticipates the 1987 UCO in a number of respects. It not only has a separate class for dwellings, but also a class for 'Residential Buildings (other than dwelling houses)' which groups together boarding houses (but apparently not hotels), blocks of flats, tenements or apartment houses, residential accommodation attached to shops and offices, residential clubs and convalescent and nursing homes. Unlike the 1987 UCO these regulations include a degree of home-based business activity in the Dwellinghouse class, and the wording is therefore of some interest:

Use Group A(c) 'Dwelling houses occupied principally as dwellings, but also used by the occupiers or tenants for professions and occupation and not used in any way as industrial buildings or for the public display of goods or for the store of bulky equipment or materials used in the occupier's profession or occupation'

Use Group A(f) 'Dwelling houses of the type described under use Class A(d) or (e)' (i.e. 'customary native design') 'but containing not more than one room used for retail trade in non-offensive commodities or handicrafts undertaken for profit; Provided that:

'1.   the primary use of the building is for a dwelling house;
'2.   the area of the room used for such retail trading or hand craft shall not exceed 120 square feet and the frontage of such room to any street shall not exceed 12 feet;
'3.   Any handcrafts undertaken shall be of such a nature as to be inaudible in neighbouring buildings'

These regulations are also interesting for their definitions of warehousing and light industry:

Use Group I (a) 'Wholesale and storage Warehouses. Wholesale and storage warehouses designed both for storage of goods and transaction of business (other than retail business) relating to such goods; storage and transit warehouses and godowns (not including storage of offensive goods or materials); furniture repositories; wholesale markets where no retail trade is carried on; including in every case, necessary offices.

Use Group M: Industrial – Service Trades. 'This Use Group covers:

'1. Small-scale industries serving the day to day needs of the local population, which

'(a) Do not employ machinery or plant which is clearly audible in the streets or in neighbouring premises under normal working conditions,

'(b) Do not employ prime movers other than manual or wind-driven machines or electric motors with a maximum individual output of 5 h.p. or a total of 20 h.p., and

'(c) Are not in any case of such a nature as to be likely to cause nuisance or annoyance to the neighbours.'

'2. Craftsman traders carried on at a scale not sufficient to warrant the provision of a factory.'

Thus one can see that the tentacles of the Use Classes Order spread far and wide.

Appendix A

The Town and Country Planning (Use Classes) Order 1987

SI 1987, No. 764

Made	*28 April 1987*
Coming into force	*1 June 1987*

The Secretary of State for the Environment, in exercise of the powers conferred on him by sections 22(2) (f) and 287(3) of the Town and Country Planning Act 1971 [1971c.78; section 22(2) (f) was amended by paragraph 1 of Schedule 11 to the Housing and Planning Act 1986 (c.63)] and of all other powers enabling him in that behalf, hereby makes the following Order:

Citation and commencement

1. This Order may be cited as the Town and Country Planning (Use Classes) Order 1987 and shall come into force on 1 June 1987.

Interpretation

2. In this Order, unless the context otherwise requires:

'care' means personal care for people in need of such care by reason of old age, disablement, past or present dependence on alcohol or drugs or past or present mental disorder, and in class C2 also includes the personal care of children and medical care and treatment;

'day centre' means premises which are visited during the day for social or recreational purposes or for the purposes of rehabilitation or occupational training, at which care is also provided;

'hazardous substance' and 'notifiable quantity' have the meaning assigned to those terms by the Notification of Installations Handling Hazardous Substances Regulations 1982 [S.I. 1982/1357];

'industrial process' means a process for or incidental to any of the following purposes:

(a) the making of any article or part of any article (including a ship or vessel, or a film, video or sound recording);

(b) the altering, repairing, maintaining, ornamenting, finishing, cleaning, washing, packing, canning, adapting for sale, breaking up or demolition of any article; or

(c) the getting, dressing or treatment of minerals;

in the course of any trade or business other than agriculture, and other than a use carried out in or adjacent to a mine or quarry;

'Schedule' means the Schedule to this Order;

'site' means the whole area of land within a single unit of occupation.

Use Classes

3. (1) Subject to the provisions of this Order, where a building or other land is used for a purpose of any class specified in the Schedule, the use of that building or that other land for any other purpose of the same class shall not be taken to involve development of the land.

(2) References in paragraph (1) to a building include references to land occupied with the building and used for the same purposes.

(3) A use which is included in and ordinarily incidental to any use in a class specified in the Schedule is not excluded from the use to which it is incidental merely because it is specified in the Schedule as a separate use.

(4) Where land on a single site or on adjacent sites used as parts of a single undertaking is used for purposes consisting of or including purposes falling within any two or more classes B1 to B7 in the Schedule, those classes may be treated as a single class in considering the use of that land for the purposes of this Order, so long as the area used for a purpose falling either within class B2 or within classes B3 to B7 is not substantially increased as a result.

(5) No class specified in the Schedule includes any use for a purpose which involves the manufacture, processing, keeping or use of a hazardous substance in such circumstances as will result in the presence at one time of a notifiable quantity of that substance in, on, over or under that building or land or any site of which that building or land forms part.

(6) No class specified in the Schedule includes use —

(a) as a theatre,

(b) as an amusement arcade or centre, or a funfair,

(c) for the washing or cleaning of clothes or fabrics in coin-operated machines or on premises at which the goods to be cleaned are received direct from the visiting public,

(d) for the sale of fuel for motor vehicles,

(e) for the sale or display for sale of motor vehicles,

(f) for a taxi business or business for the hire of motor vehicles,

(g) as a scrapyard, or a yard for the storage or distribution of minerals or the breaking of motor vehicles.

Change of use of part of building or land

4. In the case of a building used for a purpose within class C3 (dwellinghouses) in the Schedule, the use as a separate dwellinghouse of any part of the building or of any land occupied with and used for the same purposes as the building is not, by virtue of this Order, to be taken as not amounting to development.

Revocation

5. The Town and Country Planning (Use Classes) Order 1972 [S.I. 1972/1385] and the Town and Country Planning (Use Classes) (Amendment) Order 1983 [S.I. 1983/1614] are hereby revoked.

SCHEDULE

PART A

Class A1. Shops

Use for all or any of the following purposes:

- (a) for the retail sale of goods other than hot food.
- (b) as a post office.
- (c) for the sale of tickets or as a travel agency.
- (d) for the sale of sandwiches or other cold food for consumption off the premises.
- (e) for hairdressing.
- (f) for the direction of funerals.
- (g) for the display of goods for sale.
- (h) for the hiring out of domestic or personal goods or articles.
- (i) for the reception of goods to be washed, cleaned or repaired.

where the sale, display or service is to visiting members of the public.

Class A2. Financial and professional services

Use for the provision of:

- (a) financial services, or
- (b) professional services (other than health or medical services), or
- (c) any other services (including use as a betting office) which it is appropriate to provide in a shopping area,

where the services are provided principally to visiting members of the public.

Class A3. Food and drink

Use for the sale of food and drink for consumption on the premises or of hot food for consumption off the premises.

PART B

Class B1. Business

Use for all or any of the following purposes:

(a) as an office other than a use within class A2 (financial and professional services),
(b) for research and development of products or processes, or
(c) for any industrial process.

being a use which can be carried out in any residential area without detriment to the amenity of that area by reason of noise, vibration, smell, fumes, smoke, soot, ash, dust or grit.

Class B2. General industrial

Use for the carrying on of an industrial process other than one falling within class B1 above or within classes B3 to B7 below.

Class B3. Special Industrial Group A

Use for any work registrable under the Alkali, etc, Works Regulation Act 1906 and which is not included in any of classes B4 to B7 below.

Class B4. Special Industrial Group B

Use for any of the following processes, except where the process is ancillary to the getting, dressing or treatment of minerals and is carried out in or adjacent to a quarry or mine:

(a) smelting, calcining, sintering or reducing ores, minerals, concentrates or mattes;
(b) converting, refining, re-heating, annealing, hardening, melting, carburising, forging or casting metals or alloys other than pressure die-casting;
(c) recovering metal from scrap or drosses or ashes;
(d) galvanising;
(e) pickling or treating metal in acid;
(f) chromium plating.

Class B5. Special Industrial Group C

Use for any of the following processes, except where the process is ancillary to the getting, dressing or treatment of minerals and is carried on in or adjacent to a quarry or mine:

(a) burning bricks or pipes;
(b) burning lime or dolomite;
(c) producing zinc oxide, cement or alumina;

(d) foaming, crushing, screening or heating minerals or slag;

(e) processing pulverised fuel ash by heat;

(f) producing carbonate of lime or hydrated lime;

(g) producing inorganic pigments by calcining, roasting or grinding.

Class B6. Special Industrial Group D

Use for any of the following processes:

(a) distilling, refining or blending oils (other than petroleum or petroleum products);

(b) producing or using cellulose or using other pressure sprayed metal finishes (other than in vehicle repair workshops in connection with minor repairs, or the application of plastic powder by the use of fluidised bed and electrostatic spray techniques);

(c) boiling linseed oil or running gum;

(d) processes involving the use of hot pitch or bitumen (except the use of bitumen in the manufacture of roofing felt at temperatures not exceeding 220°C and also the manufacture of coated roadstone);

(e) stoving enamelled ware;

(f) producing aliphatic esters of the lower fatty acids, butyric acid, caramel, hexamine, iodoform, naphthols, resin products (excluding plastic moulding or extrusion operations and producing plastic sheets, rods, tubes, filaments, fibres or optical components produced by casting, calendering, moulding, shaping or extrusion), salicylic acid or sulphonated organic compounds;

(g) producing rubber from scrap;

(h) chemical processes in which chlorophenols or chlorocresols are used as intermediates;

(i) manufacturing acetylene from calcium carbide;

(j) manufacturing, recovering or using pyridine or picolines, any methyl or ethyl amine or acrylates.

Class B7. Special Industrial Group E

Use for carrying on any of the following industries, businesses or trades:

Boiling blood, chitterlings, nettlings or soap.

Boiling, burning, grinding or steaming bones.

Boiling or cleaning tripe.

Breeding maggots from putrescible animal matter.

Cleaning, adapting or treating animal hair.

Curing fish.

Dealing in rags and bones (including receiving, storing, sorting or manipulating rags in, or likely to become in, an offensive condition, or any bones, rabbit skins, fat or putrescible animal products of a similar nature).

Dressing or scraping fish skins.

Drying skins.

Making manure from bones, fish, offal, blood, spent hops, beans or other putrescible animal or vegetable matter.

Making or scraping guts.

Manufacturing animal charcoal, blood albumen, candles, catgut, glue, fish oil, size or feeding stuff for animals or poultry from meat, fish, blood, bone, feathers, fat or animal offal either in an offensive condition or subjected to any process causing noxious or injurious effluvia.

Melting, refining or extracting fat or tallow.

Preparing skins for working.

Class B8. Storage or distribution

Use for storage or as a distribution centre.

PART C

Class C1. Hotels and hostels

Use as a hotel, boarding or guest house or as a hotel or as a hostel where, in each case, no significant element of care is provided.

Class C2. Residential institutions

Use for the provision of residential accommodation and care to people in need of care (other than a use within class C3 (dwelling houses)).

Use as a hospital or nursing home.

Use as a residential school, college or training centre.

Class C3. Dwellinghouses

Use as a dwellinghouse (whether or not as a sole or main residence):

(a) by a single person or by people living together as a family, or
(b) by not more than 6 residents living together as a single household (including a household where care is provided for residents).

PART D

Class D1. Non-residential institutions

Any use not including a residential use:

(a) for the provision of any medical or health services except the use of premises attached to the residence of the consultant or practitioner,

(b) as a crèche, day nursery or day centre,

(c) for the provision of education,

(d) for the display of works of art (otherwise than for sale or hire),

(e) as a museum,

(f) as a public library or public reading room,

(g) as a public hall or exhibition hall,

(h) for, or in connection with, public worship or religious instruction.

Class D2. Assembly and leisure

Use as:

(a) a cinema,

(b) a concert hall,

(c) a bingo hall or casino,

(d) a dance hall,

(e) a swimming bath, skating rink, gymnasium or area for other indoor or outdoor sports or recreations, not involving motorised vehicles or firearms.

Nicholas Ridley
Secretary of State for the Environment

28 April 1987

Appendix B

Town and Country Planning (Use Classes for Third Schedule Purposes) Order 1948

SI 1948, No. 955

Dated 8 May 1948, made by the Minister of Town and Country Planning under the Town and Country Planning Act 1947, Sched. III, para. 6.

Citation

1. This Order may be cited as the Town and Country Planning (Use Classes for Third Schedule Purposes) Order 1948.

Interpretation

2.—(1) The Interpretation Act 1889 shall apply to the interpretation of this Order as it applies to the interpretation of an Act of Parliament.

(2) In this Order, unless the context otherwise requires, the following expressions have the meanings respectively assigned to them, namely —

'the Act' means the Town and Country Planning Act 1947;

'shop' means a building used for the carrying on of any retail trade or retail business wherein the primary purpose is the selling of goods (excluding refreshments other than light refreshments) by retail, and without prejudice to the generality of the foregoing includes a building used for the purposes of a hairdresser, undertaker, ticket agency or receiving office for goods to be washed, cleaned or repaired, or for other purposes appropriate to a shopping area, but does not include a building used as an amusement arcade, pin-table saloon, funfair, garage, petrol filling station, hotel or premises licensed for the sale of intoxicating liquors for consumption on the premises;

'light refreshments' means eatables not cooked on the premises, and beverages;

'building' includes part of a building;

'office' includes a bank;

'industrial building' means a building (other than a building in or adjacent to and belonging to a quarry or mine and other than a shop) used for the carrying on of any process for or incidental to any of the following purposes, namely —

(a) the making of any article or part of any article, or

(b) the altering, repairing, ornamenting, finishing, cleaning, washing, packing or canning, or adapting for sale, or breaking up or demolition of any article, or

(c) without prejudice to the foregoing paragraphs, the getting, dressing or treatment of minerals,

being in process carried on in the course of trade or business other than agriculture, and for the purposes of this definition the expression 'article' means an article of any description, including a ship or vessel;

'light industrial building' means an industrial building (not being a special industrial building) in which the processes carried on or the machinery installed are such as could be carried on or installed in any residential area without detriment to the amenity of that area by reason of noise, vibration, smell, fumes, smoke, soot, ash, dust or grit;

'general industrial building' means an industrial building other than a light industrial building or a special industrial building;

'special industrial building' means an industrial building used for one or more of the purposes specified in Classes V, VI, VII, VIII, and IX referred to in the Schedule to this Order;

'wholesale warehouse' means a building where business, principally of a wholesale nature, is transacted and goods are stored or displayed, but only incidentally to the transaction of that business;

'repository' means a building (excluding any land occupied therewith) where storage is the principal use and where no business is transacted other than incidentally to such storage;

and references to a building may, except where otherwise provided, include references to land occupied therewith and used for the same purposes.

Use Classes

3.—(1) The classes specified in the schedule to this Order, shall be the general classes for the purposes of paragraph 6 of the Third Schedule to the Act.

(2) Where a group of contiguous or adjacent buildings used as parts of a single undertaking includes industrial buildings used for purposes falling within two or more of the classes specified in the Schedule to this Order as Classes III to IX inclusive, those particular two or more classes may, in relation to that group of buildings, and so long as the area occupied in that group by either general or special industrial buildings is not substantially increased thereby be treated as a single class for the purposes of this Order.

(3) A use which is ordinarily incidental to and included in any use specified in the Schedule to this Order is not excluded from that use as an incident thereto merely by reason of its specification in the said Schedule as a separate use.

SCHEDULE

Class I. — Use as a shop for any purpose except as:
  (i)   a fried fish shop;
  (ii) a tripe shop;
  (iii) a shop for the sale of pet animals or birds;
  (iv) a cats-meat shop.

Class II. — Use as an office for any purpose.

Class III. — Use as a light industrial building for any purpose.

Class IV. — Use as a general industrial building for any purpose.

Class V. (Special Industrial Group A) — Use for any work which is registrable under the Alkali etc. Works Regulation Act 1906, as extended by the Alkali etc. Works Orders 1928 to 1939 [S.R. & O. 1928, No. 26; 1935, No. 162; 1939, No. 1229], except a process ancillary to the getting, dressing or treatment of minerals, carried on in or adjacent to a quarry or mine.

Use for any of the following processes, except as aforesaid, so far as not registrable under the above Act:
  (i)   smelting, calcining, sintering or other reduction of ores or minerals;
  (ii) converting, reheating, annealing, hardening or carburising, forging or casting, of iron or other metals;
  (iii) galvanising;
  (iv) recovering of metal from scrap;
  (v)   pickling or treatment of metal in acid;
  (vi) chromium plating.

Class VI. (Special Industrial Group B) — Use for any of the following processes so far as not included in Class V and except a process ancillary to the getting, dressing or treatment of minerals, carried on in or adjacent to a quarry or mine:
  (i)   burning of building bricks;
  (ii) lime and dolomite burning;
  (iii) carbonisation of coal in coke ovens;
  (iv) production of calcium carbide, lampblack or zinc oxide;
  (v)   crushing or screening of stone or slag.

Class VII. (Special Industrial Group C) — Use for any of the following purposes so far as not included in Class V:

The production or employment of
  (i)   cyanogen or its compounds;
  (ii) liquid or gaseous sulphur dioxide;
  (iii) sulphur chlorides.

Salt glazing.

Sintering of sulphur bearing materials.

The manufacture of glass, where the sodium sulphate used exceeds 1.5 per cent of the total weight of the melt.

The production of ultramarine or zinc chloride.

Class VIII. (Special Industrial Group D) — Use for any of the following purposes, so far as not included in Class V:

The distilling, refining or blending of oils, the production or employment of cellulose lacquers (except their employment in garages in connection with minor repairs), hot pitch or bitumen, or pyridine; the stoving of enamelled ware; the production of amyl acetate, aromatic esters, butyric acid, caramel, hexamine, iodoform, B-naphthol, resin products (except synthetic resins, plastic moulding or extrusion compositions and plastic sheets, rods, tubes, filaments, fibres or optical components produced by casting, calendering, moulding, shaping or extrusion), salicylic acid, or sulphonated organic compounds; paint and varnish manufacture (excluding mixing, milling and grinding); the production of rubber from scrap; or the manufacture of acetylene from calcium carbide, for sale or for use in further chemical process.

Class IX. (Special Industrial Group E) — Use for carrying on any of the following industries, businesses or trades so far as not included in Class V:

Animal charcoal manufacturer.

Blood albumen maker.

Blood boiler.

Bone boiler or steamer.

Bone burner.

Bone grinder.

Breeder of maggots from putrescible animal matter.

Candle maker.

Catgut manufacturer.

Chitterling or nettlings boiler.

Dealer in rags or bones (including receiving, storing, sorting or manipulating rags in or likely to become in an offensive condition, or any bones, rabbit-skins, fat or putrescible animal products of a like nature).

Fat melter or fat extractor.

Fellmonger.

Fish curer.

Fish oil manufacturer.

Fish skin dresser or scraper.

Glue maker.

Gut scraper or gut cleaner.

Leather dresser.

Maker of meal for feeding poultry, dogs, cattle, or other animals from any fish, blood, bone, fat or animal offal, either in an offensive condition or subjected to any process causing noxious or injurious effluvia.

Manufacturer of manure from bones, fish, fish offal, blood, spent hops, beans or other putrescible animal or vegetable matter.

Parchment maker.

Size maker.

Skin drier.

Soap boiler.

Tallow melter or refiner.

Tanner.

Tripe boiler or cleaner.

Class X. — Use as a wholesale warehouse for any purpose, except storage of offensive or dangerous goods.

Class XI. — Use as a repository for any purpose except storage of offensive or dangerous goods.

Class XII. — Use as a building for public worship or religious instruction or for the social or recreational activities of the religious body using the building.

Class XIII. — Use as a residential or boarding schcol, a residential college, an orphanage or a home or institution providing for the boarding, care and maintenance of children (other than a hospital, home, hostel, or institution included in Class XVII or Class XVIII).

Class XIV. — Use as a boarding or guest house, a residential club, a hostel or a hotel providing sleeping accommodation.

Class XV. — Use (other than for persons of unsound mind, mental defectives or epileptic persons) as a convalescent home, a nursing home, a sanatorium or a hospital.

Class XVI. — Use (other than residentially) as a health centre, a school treatment centre, a clinic, a crèche, a day nursery or a dispensary, or use as a consulting room or surgery unattached to the residence of the consultant or practitioner.

Class XVII. — Use as a hospital, home or institution for persons of unsound mind, mental defectives, or epileptic persons.

Class XVIII. — Use as a home, hostel or institution in which persons may be detained by order of a court or which is approved by one of His Majesty's Principal Secretaries of State for persons required to reside there as a condition of a probation or a supervision order.

Class XIX. — Use as a theatre, a cinema or a music hall.

Class XX. — Use as an art gallery (other than for business purposes), a museum, a public library or as a public reading room.

Class XXI. — Use as a dance hall, a skating rink, a swimming bath, a turkish or other vapour or foam bath or a gymnasium, or for indoor games.

Class XXII. — Use as a public hall, a concert hall, an exhibition hall, a social centre, a community centre or a non-residential club.

Appendix C

The Town and Country Planning (Use Classes) Order 1972

SI 1972, No. 1385

Made   11 September 1972
Coming into operation   23 October 1972

The Secretary of State for the Environment, in exercise of the powers conferred on him by section 22 of the Town and Country Planning Act 1971 and of all other powers enabling him in that behalf, hereby makes the following order:

Citation and commencement
1.   This Order may be cited as the Town and Country Planning (Use Classes) Order 1972 and shall come into operation on 23 October 1972.

Interpretation
2.—(1) The Interpretation Act 1889 shall apply to the interpretation of this Order as it applies to the interpretation of an Act of Parliament.

(2) In this Order —

'the Act' means the Town and Country Planning Act 1971;

'shop' means a building used for the carrying on of any retail trade or retail business wherein the primary purpose is the selling of goods by retail, and includes a building used for the purposes of a hairdresser, undertaker, ticket agency or post office or for the reception of goods to be washed, cleaned or repaired, or for other purposes appropriate to a shopping area, but does not include a building used as a fun-fair, amusement arcade, pin-table saloon, garage, launderette, petrol filling station, office, betting office, hotel, restaurant, snackbar or café or premises licenced for the sale of intoxicating liquors for consumption on the premises;

'office' includes a bank and premises occupied by an estate agency, building society or employment agency, or (for office purposes only) for the business of car hire or driving instruction but does not include a post office or betting office;

'post office' does not include any building in respect of which there is for the time being in force a betting office licence pursuant to the provisions of the Betting and Gaming Act 1960;

'launderette' includes any building used for the purpose of washing or cleaning clothes or fabrics in coin-operated machines;

'industrial building' means a building (other than a building in or adjacent to and belonging to a quarry or mine and other than a shop) used for the carrying on of any process for or incidental to any of the following purposes, namely —

(a) the making of any article or part of any article, or
(b) the altering, repairing, ornamenting, finishing, cleaning, washing, packing or canning, or adapting for sale, or breaking up or demolition of any article, or
(c) without prejudice to the foregoing paragraphs, the getting, dressing or treatment of minerals,

being a process carried on in the course of trade or business other than agriculture, and for the purposes of this definition the expression 'article' means an article of any description, including a ship or vessel;

'light industrial building' means an industrial building (not being a special industrial building) in which the processes carried on or the machinery installed are such as could be carried on or installed in any residential area without detriment to the amenity of that area by reason of noise, vibration, smell, fumes, smoke, soot, ash, dust or grit;

'general industrial building' means an industrial building other than a light industrial building or a special industrial building;

'special industrial building' means an industrial building used for one or more of the purposes specified in Classes V, VI, VII, VIII, and IX referred to in the Schedule to this order;

'motor vehicle' means any motor vehicle for the purposes of the Road Traffic Act 1960.

(3) References in this order to a building may, except where otherwise provided, include references to land occupied therewith and used for the same purposes.

Use Classes

3.—(1) Where a building or other land is used for the purpose of any class specified in the Schedule to this order, the use of such a building or other land for any other purpose of the same class shall not be deemed for the purposes of the Act to involve development of the land.

(2) Where a group of contiguous or adjacent buildings used as parts of a single undertaking includes industrial buildings used for purposes falling within two or more of the classes specified in the Schedule to this order as Classes III to IX inclusive, those particular two or more classes may, in relation to that group of buildings, and so long as the area occupied in that

group by either general or special industrial buildings is not substantially increased thereby be treated as a single class for the purposes of this order.

(3) A use which is ordinarily incidental to and included in any use specified in the Schedule to this order is not excluded from that use as an incident thereto merely by reason of its specification in the said Schedule as a separate use.

Revocation

4. The Town and Country Planning (Use Classes) Order 1963 [S.I. 1963/708] and the Town and Country Planning (Use Classes) (Amendment) Order 1965 [S.I. 1965/229] are hereby revoked.

SCHEDULE

Class I. — Use as a shop for any purpose except as:
 (i) a shop for the sale of hot food;
 (ii) a tripe shop;
 (iii) a shop for the sale of pet animals or birds;
 (iv) a cats-meat shop.
 (v) a shop for the sale of motor vehicles.

Class II. — Use as an office for any purpose.

Class III. — Use as a light industrial building for any purpose.

Class IV. — Use as a general industrial building for any purpose.

Class V. (Special Industrial Group A) — Use for any work which is registrable under the Alkali etc. Works Regulation Act 1906 as extended by the Alkali etc. Works Orders 1966 and 1971 [S.I. 1966/1143, 1971/960] and which is not included in any of the Classes VI, VII, VIII or IX of this Schedule.

Class VI. (Special Industrial Group B) — Use for any of the following processes, except a process ancillary to the getting, dressing or treatment of minerals which is carried on in or adjacent to a quarry or mine:

 (i) smelting, calcining, sintering or other reduction of ores, minerals concentrates or mattes;
 (ii) converting, refining, re-heating, annealing, hardening, melting, carburising, forging or casting of metals or alloys, other than pressure die-casting;
 (iii) recovery of metal from scrap or drosses or ashes;
 (iv) galvanising;
 (v) pickling or treatment of metal in acid;
 (vi) chromium plating.

Class VII. (Special Industrial Group C) — Use for any of the following processes except a process ancillary to the getting, dressing or treatment of minerals which is carried on in or adjacent to a quarry or mine:
 (i) burning of bricks or pipes;
 (ii) lime or dolomite burning;

    (iii)   production of zinc oxide, cement or alumina;

    (iv)   foaming, crushing, screening or heating of minerals or slag;

    (v)   processing by heat of pulverised fuel ash;

    (vi)   production of carbonate of lime and hydrated lime;

    (vii)   production of inorganic pigments by calcining, roasting or grinding.

Class VIII. (Special Interest Group D) — Use for any of the following purposes:

    (i)   distilling, refining or blending of oils (other than petroleum or petroleum products;

    (ii)   production or employment of cellulose and employment of other pressure sprayed metal finishes (other than the employment of any such finishes in vehicle repair workshops in connection with minor repairs, and the application of plastic powder by the use of fluidised bed and electrostatic spray techniques);

    (iii)   boiling of linseed oil and the running of gum;

    (iv)   processes involving the use of hot pitch or bitumen (except the use of bitumen in the manufacture of roofing felt at temperatures not exceeding 220°C and also the manufacture of coated roadstone);

    (v)   stoving of enamelled ware;

    (vi)   production of aliphatic esters of the lower fatty acids, butyric acid, caramel, hexamine, iodoform, naphthols, resin products (excluding plastic moulding or extrusion operations and production of plastic sheets, rods, tubes, filaments, fibres or optical components produced by casting, calendering, moulding, shaping or extrusion), salicylic acid or sulphonated organic compounds;

    (vii)   production of rubber from scrap;

    (viii)   chemical processes in which chlorophenols or chlorocresols are used as intermediates;

    (ix)   manufacture of acetylene from calcium carbide;

    (x)   manufacture, recovery or use of pyridine or picolines, any methyl or ethyl amine or acrylates.

Class IX. (Special Industrial Group E) — Use for carrying on any of the following industries, businesses or trades:

Animal charcoal manufacturer.

Animal hair cleanser, adaptor or treater.

Blood albumen maker.

Blood boiler.

Bone boiler or steamer.

Bone burner.

Bone grinder.

Breeder of maggots from putrescible animal matter.

Candle maker.

Catgut manufacturer.

Chitterling or nettlings boiler.

Dealer in rags or bones (including receiving, storing, sorting or manipulating rags in or likely to become in an offensive condition, or any bones, rabbit-skins, fat or putrescible animal products of a like nature).

Fat melter or fat extractor.

Fellmonger.

Fish curer.

Fish oil manufacturer.

Fish skin dresser or scraper.

Glue maker.

Gut scraper or gut cleaner.

Maker of feeding stuff for animals or poultry from any meat, fish, blood, bone, feathers, fat or animal offal, either in an offensive condition or subjected to any process causing noxious or injurious effluvia.

Manufacture of manure from bones, fish, offal, blood, spent hops, beans or other putrescible animal or vegetable matter.

Size maker.

Skin drier.

Soap boiler.

Tallow melter or refiner.

Tripe boiler or cleaner.

Class X. — Use as a wholesale warehouse or repository for any purpose.

Class XI. — Use as a boarding or guest house, or an hotel providing sleeping accommodation.

Class XII. — Use as a residential or boarding school or a residential college.

Class XIII. — Use as a building for public worship or religious instruction or for the social or recreational activities of the religious body using the building.

Class XIV. — Use as a home or institution providing for the boarding care and maintenance of children, old people or persons under disability, a convalescent home, a nursing home, a sanatorium or a hospital.

Class XV. — Use (other than residentially) as a health centre, a school treatment centre, a clinic, a crèche, a day nursery or a dispensary, or use as a consulting room or surgery unattached to the residence of the consultant or practitioner.

Class XVI. — Use as an art gallery, (other than for business purposes), a museum, a public library or reading room, a public hall, or an exhibition hall.

Class XVII. — Use as theatre, cinema, music hall or concert hall.
Class XVIII. — Use as a dance hall, skating rink, swimming bath, Turkish or other vapour or foam bath, or as a gymnasium or sports hall.

P. Walker
11 September 1972　　　　　Secretary of State for the Environment

Appendix D

Property Advisory Group Recommendations (PAG 1985)

1. Shops

(A) The definition of 'shop' in Article 2(2) of the UCO should exclude the reference to 'any other purpose appropriate to a shopping area'.

(B) The definition should include launderettes, betting offices, restaurants, snack bars, cafés, showrooms and buildings used for the hiring out of domestic or personal goods or articles. (Para. 6.06)

(C) Banks, estate agencies, building societies and employment agencies should be transferred from the definition of 'office' (Class II) and added to the definition of 'shop'. (Para. 6.08)

(D) Exceptions (i) to (v) inclusive in Use Class I should be removed. (Para. 6.05)

(E) (Majority Recommendation) The definition of 'shop' should also include certain types of office in which the activity carried on consists of the provision of personal services to members of the public. (Para. 6.12)

2. Offices, light industry and other business uses

A new use class should be created by amalgamating Use Classes II (offices) and III (light industrial buildings) and incorporating certain additional business activities which at present are or may arguably be *sui generis* uses but are comparable in their impact on the environment and general commercial character to offices and light industry. These additional uses should be included by being expressly specified in the UCO rather than by general words of definition or exclusion (para. 7.09). Some of those *sui generis* uses which might be included within this new class are referred to in para. 7.09.

3. Residential institutions

A new single use class should be created which would combine the existing Classes XI (boarding or guest houses and hotels), XII (residential schools and colleges) and XIV (houses and institutions providing care for children, old people and others), and include the use of premises as a hostel (para. 10.01).

4. Non-residential institutions
A new single use class should be created which would combine the existing Classes XV (health and day centres etc.) and XVI (art galleries, museums etc.) and include the use of premises as a non-residential school or college (para. 10.02).

5. Places of assembly and public resort
A new class should be created to include the use of premises for any purpose comprised within the existing Use Classes XIII (places of worship etc.), XVII (theatres, cinemas etc.) and XVIII (dance halls, skating rinks etc.). This new class should also include sporting activities generally and other leisure uses (para. 10.03).

6. Residential premises
A new use class should be created to cover the use of a building for the purposes of a residence. This use should expressly include the use of a building by any resident concurrently with his or her occupation of the property for any activity compatible with that principal use, which (1) can be carried on in any residential area without detriment to the amenity of that area by reason of noise, vibration, smell, fumes, smoke, soot, ash, dust or grit; (2) does not generate vehicular traffic of a type or amount which is detrimental to the amenity of the area in which it is conducted; and (3) does not involve the presence on the premises of more than five persons engaged in business (including the proprietors) at any one time (para. 11.09). The new class should also include the provision of permanent housing accommodation for certain people in premises not falling within Use Class XIV (as amended) (para. 11.10).

7. Sub-division of units
Any re-draft of the UCO should enable a single planning unit currently in use for a purpose falling within a use class to be sub-divided into two or more separate units to be devoted to a use or uses falling within the same class without the necessity of obtaining planning permission. (If necessary, the 1971 Act should also be amended to allow that kind of sub-division to take place.) (para. 12.09)

8. Open land
Three new classes should be introduced to cover the use of open land for (1) the sale of any goods by retail; (2) light industrial purposes (as at present defined); and (3) general industrial purposes (as at present defined). (para. 13.03)

PART 2: OTHER RECOMMENDATIONS

9. The Secretary of State should give further guidance to planning authorities on the concept of ancillary uses (para. 5.04).

10. When the Simplified Planning Zone procedure is introduced, planning authorities should be advised that it should be used wherever possible to enlarge upon the basic freedom from control which is conferred by the UCO. (para. 5.05)

11. Consultations should be held to discover whether any new uses ought to be added to the Special Industrial Use Classes (Classes V to IX) and whether some freedom of interchange between those Classes should be allowed by the making of a Development Order. (paras. 8.03 and 8.04)

12. Freedom of change from warehouse use to any use comprised in the new use class recommended in para. 2 of this Appendix should be allowed by the making of a general development order; and the new Simplified Planning Zone procedure should be utilised to bring about the complete amalgamation of warehouse use with that new class in areas where it is appropriate to do so. (para. 9.03)

13. Section 22(3) of the 1971 Act, which provides that the sub-division of one separate dwelling into two (or more) amounts to development, should be repealed. (para. 11.10)

14. When a new UCO is made, the Secretary of State will have to give guidance to planning authorities on the effect which it ought to have on their approach to applications for permission to carry out building or engineering operations, and on a wide range of other planning questions. (paras. 14.02–14.04)

Appendix E

The Town and Country Planning (Use Classes) (Scotland) Order 1989

Made   *27th January 1989*
Coming into force   *27th March 1989*

The Secretary of State, in exercise of the powers conferred on him by sections 19(2)(f) and 273(3) of the Town and Country Planning (Scotland) Act 1972 and of all other powers enabling him in that behalf hereby makes the following Order:

Citation and commencement

1. This order may be cited as the Town and Country Planning (Use Classes) (Scotland) Order 1989 and shall come into force on 27 March 1989.

Interpretation

2. In this Order, the following expressions have the meanings assigned to them:—

'care' means personal care including the provision of appropriate help with physical and social needs or support: and in class 13 (residential institutions) includes medical care and treatment;

'class' means a class specified in the Schedule to this Order;

'day centre' means non-residential premises which are used for social purposes, recreation, rehabilitation or occupational training and at which care is also provided;

'hazardous substance' and 'notifiable quantity' have the meanings assigned to those terms by the Notification of Installations Handling Hazardous Substances Regulations 1982(**b**);

'industrial process' means a process, other than a process carried out in or adjacent to, a mine or quarry, for or incidental to:

(a) the making of any article or part of any article including a ship or vessel or a film, video or sound recording;

(b) the altering, repairing, maintaining, ornamenting, finishing, cleaning, washing, packing, canning, adapting for sale, breaking up or demolition of any article; or

(c) the getting, dressing or treatment of minerals; in the course of any use other than agriculture;

'site' means the whole area of land within a single unit of occupation;

'support' means counselling or other help provided as part of a planned programme of care.

Use Classes

3.—(1) Subject to the provisions of this Order, where a building or other land is used for a purpose in any class specified in the Schedule to this Order, the use of that building or that other land for any other purpose in the same class shall not be taken to involve development of the land.

(2) References in paragraph (1) to the building include references to land occupied with the building and used for the same purposes.

(3) A use included in and ordinarily incidental to any use in a class shall not be precluded from that use by virtue of being specified in another class.

(4) Where land on a single site or on adjacent sites used as parts of a single undertaking comprises uses within any two or more of classes 4 to 10 (business and industrial groups), those uses may be treated as if they were in a single class in considering the use of that land for the purposes of this Order, provided that the area used for a purpose falling either within class 5 (general industrial) or within classes 6 to 10 (special industrial groups) shall not be substantially increased as a result.

(5) Nothing in any class shall include any use—
  (a) as a theatre;
  (b) as an amusement arcade or centre, or funfair;
  (c) for the sale of fuel for motor vehicles;
  (d) for the sale or display for sale of motor vehicles;
  (e) for a taxi business or for the hire of motor vehicles;
  (f) as a scrapyard, or a yard for the breaking of motor vehicles;
  (g) for the storage or distribution of minerals;
  (h) as a public house; or
  (i) of a building or other land involving the manufacturing, processing, keeping or use of a hazardous substance which will cause there to be at any one time a notifiable quantity of that substance in, on, over or under that building or land or any site of which that building or land forms part.

Change of use of part of building or land

4. In the case of a building used for a purpose within class 14 (houses) the use as a separate house of any part of the building or of any land occupied with and used for the same purposes as the building shall not, by virtue of this Order, be taken as not amounting to development.

Revocation

5. The Town and Country Planning (Use Classes) (Scotland) Order 1973 and the Town and Country Planning (Use Classes) (Scotland) Amendment Order 1983 are hereby revoked.

James Douglas-Hamilton
St. Andrew's House, Edinburgh   Parliamentary Under Secretary of State,
27 January 1989   Scottish Office

SCHEDULE Regulation 3

Class I. Shops
Use
  (a) for the retail sale of goods other than hot food;
  (b) as a post office;
  (c) for the sale of tickets;
  (d) as a travel agency;
  (e) for the sale of cold food for consumption off the premises;
  (f) for hairdressing;
  (g) for the direction of funerals;
  (h) for the display of goods for sale;
  (i) for the hiring out of domestic or personal goods or articles;
  (j) as a launderette or dry cleaners; or
  (k) for the reception of goods to be washed, cleaned or repaired;
where the sale, display or service is principally to visiting members of the public.

Class 2. Financial, professional and other services
Use for the provision of—
  (a) financial services;
  (b) professional services;
  (c) any other services (including use as a betting office);
which it is appropriate to provide in a shopping area and where the services are provided principally to visiting members of the public.

Class 3. Food and Drink
Use for the sale of food or drink for consumption on the premises or of hot food for consumption off the premises.

Class 4. Business
Use—
  (a) as an office, other than a use within class 2 (financial, professional and other services);
  (b) for research and development of products or processes; or
  (c) for any industrial process;
being a use which can be carried on in any residential area without detriment to the amenity of that area by reason of noise, vibration, smell, fumes, smoke, soot, ash, dust or grit.

Class 5. General industrial
Use for the carrying on of an industrial process other than one falling within class 4 (business) or within classes 6 to 10 (special industrial groups).

Class 6. Special industrial group A

Use for any work registrable under the Alkali etc. Works Regulation Act 1906, and which is not included in any of classes 7 to 10 (special industrial groups B to E).

Class 7. Special industrial group B

Use for—

  (a) smelting, calcining, sintering or reducing ores, minerals, concentrates or mattes;

  (b) converting, refining, re-heating, annealing, hardening, melting, carburising, forging or casting metals or alloys other than pressure die-casting;

  (c) recovering of metal from scrap or drosses or ashes;

  (d) galvanising;

  (e) pickling or treating metal in acid; or

  (f) chromium plating;

other than where the process is ancillary to the getting, dressing or treatment of minerals and is carried on in or adjacent to, a quarry or mine.

Class 8. Special industrial group C

Use for—

  (a) burning bricks or pipes;

  (b) burning lime or dolomite;

  (c) producing zinc oxide, cement or alumina;

  (d) foaming, crushing, screening or heating mineral or slag;

  (e) processing pulverised fuel ash by heat;

  (f) producing carbonate of lime or hydrated lime; or

  (g) producing inorganic pigments by calcining, roasting or grinding,

other than where the process is ancillary to the getting, dressing or treatment of minerals and is carried on in or adjacent to, a quarry or mine.

Class 9. Special industrial group D

Use for—

  (a) distilling, refining or blending oils other than petroleum or petroleum products;

  (b) producing or using cellulose or using other pressure sprayed metal finishes other than in—

    (i) vehicle repair workshops in connection with minor repairs, or

    (ii) the application of plastic powder by the use of fluidised bed and electrostatic spray techniques;

  (c) boiling linseed oil or running gum;

  (d) processes involving the use of hot pitch or bitumen, except the use of bitumen in the manufacture of—

    (i) roofing felt at temperatures not exceeding 220C, or

    (ii) coated roadstone;

(e)   stoving enamelled ware;
(f)   producing—
        (i)   aliphatic esters of the lower fatty acids,
        (ii) butyric acid or salicylic acid,
        (iii) caramel, hexamine, iodoform or naphthols,
        (iv) sulphonated organic compounds, or
        (v)   resin products other than the manufacture of plastic goods;
(g)   producing rubber from scrap;
(h)   chemical processes in which chlorophenols or chlorocresols are used as
        intermediates;
(i)   manufacturing acetylene from calcium carbide; or
(j)   manufacturing, recovering or using
        (i)   pyridine or picolines,
        (ii) any methyl or ethyl amine, or
        (iii) acrylates.

Class 10. Special industrial group E

Use for—
(a)   boiling blood, chitterlings, nettlings or soap;
(b)   boiling, burning, grinding or steaming bones;
(c)   boiling or cleaning tripe;
(d)   breeding maggots from putrescrible animal matter;
(e)   cleaning, adapting or treating animal hair;
(f)   curing fish;
(g)   dealing in rags or bones, including receiving, storing, sorting or
        manipulating rags in, or likely to become in, an offensive condition, or
        any bones, rabbit skins, fat or putrescrible animal products of a similar
        nature;
(h)   dressing or scraping fish skins;
(i)   drying skins;
(j)   making manure from bones, fish, offal, blood, spent hops, beans or
        other putrescrible animal or vegetable matter;
(k)   cleaning or scraping guts;
(l)   manufacturing animal charcoal, blood albumen, candles, catgut, glue,
        fish oil, size or feeding stuff for animals or for poultry from meat, fish,
        blood, bone, feathers, fat or animal offal either in an offensive
        condition or subjected to any process causing noxious or injurious
        effluvia;
(m)   melting, refining or extracting fat or tallow; or
(n)   preparing skins for working.

Class 11. Storage or distribution

Use for storage or as a distribution centre.

Class 12. Hotels and hostels

Use as a hotel, boarding house, guest house, or hostel where no significant element of care is provided, other than premises licensed for the sale of alcoholic liquor to persons other than residents or to persons other than persons consuming meals on the premises.

Class 13. Residential institutions

Use—
- (a) for the provision of residential accommodation and care to people in need of care other than a use within class 14 (houses);
- (b) as a hospital or nursing home; or
- (c) as a residential school, college or training centre.

Class 14. Houses

Use as a house, other than a flat, whether or not as a sole or main residence, by—
- (a) a single person or by people living together as a family, or
- (b) not more than 5 residents living together including a household where care is provided for residents.

Class 15. Non-residential institutions

Use, not including residential use,—
- (a) as a crèche, day nursery or day centre;
- (b) for the provision of education;
- (c) for the display of works of art (otherwise than for sale or hire);
- (d) as a museum;
- (e) as a public library or public reading room;
- (f) as a public hall or exhibition hall; or
- (g) for, or in connection with, public worship or religious instruction, or the social or recreational activities of a religious body.

Class 16. Assembly and leisure

Use as a—
- (a) cinema;
- (b) concert hall;
- (c) bingo hall or casino;
- (d) dance hall or discotheque; or
- (e) swimming bath, skating rink, gymnasium or area for other indoor or outdoor sports or recreation, not involving motorised vehicles or firearms.

Appendix F

Irish Local Government (Planning and Development) Act 1963, Third Schedule

PART IV: CLASSES OF USE

CLASS *1* – Use as a shop for any purpose except as—
  (a) a fried fish shop or a shop for the sale of hot food for consumption off the premises.
  (b) a shop for the sale of pet animals or birds,
  (c) a shop for the sale or display for sale of motor vehicles other than bicycles.

CLASS *2* – Use as an office for any purpose.

CLASS *3* – Use as a light industrial building for any purpose.

CLASS *4* – Use as a general industrial building for any purpose.

CLASS *5* – Use for any work which is registrable under the Alkali, etc. Works Regulation Act, 1906, except a process ancillary to the getting, dressing or treatment of minerals, carried on in or adjacent to a quarry or mine; use for any of the following processes, except as aforesaid, so far as not registrable under the above Act:—
  (a) smelting, calcining, sintering or reduction of ores, minerals, concentrates or mattes,
  (b) converting, reheating, annealing, hardening, melting, carburising, forging or casting of iron or other metals or alloys.
  (c) recovering of metal from scrap or drosses or ashes,
  (d) galvanising
  (e) pickling or treatment of metal in acid
  (f) chromium plating.

CLASS *6* – Use for any of the following processes so far as not included in class 5 of this Part of this Schedule and except a process ancillary to the getting, dressing or treatment of minerals, carried on in or adjacent to a quarry or mine—
  (a) burning of building bricks,
  (b) lime burning,
  (c) production of calcium carbide or zinc oxide,
  (d) foaming, crushing or screening of stone or slag.

CLASS *7* – Use for any of the following purposes so far as not included in class 5 of this Part of this Schedule—

(a) the production or employment of cyanogen or its compounds,

(b) the manufacture of glass, where the sodium sulphate used exceeds 1.5 per cent of the total weight of the melt,

(c) the production of zinc chloride.

CLASS 8 – Use for any of the following purposes so far as not included in class 5 of this Part of this Schedule—

The distilling, refining or blending of oils, the production or employment of cellulose lacquers (except their employment in garages in connection with minor repairs), hot pitch or bitumen or pyridine; the stoving of enamelled ware; the production of amyl acetate, aromatic esters, butyric acid, caramel, hexamine, iodoform, B-naphthol, resin products (except synthetic resins, plastic moulding or extrusion compositions and plastic sheets, rods, tubes, filaments, fibres or optical components produced by casting, calendering, moulding, shaping or extrusion), salicylic acid or sulphonated organic compounds; paint and varnish manufacture (excluding mixing, milling and grinding); the production of rubber from scrap; or the manufacture of acetylene from calcium carbide for sale or for use in a further chemical process.

CLASS 9 – Use as a wholesale warehouse or enclosed respository building for any purpose.

CLASS 10 – Use as a residential club, a hotel providing sleeping accommodation, a guest house or a hostel.

CLASS 11 – Use as a structure for public worship or religious instruction; use of such structure for the social or recreational activities of the religious body using the structure; as a monastery or convent,

CLASS 12 – Use as a residential or boarding school or a residential college.

CLASS 13 – Use as a convalescent home, a maternity home, a nursing home, a sanatorium, a hospital, a health centre, a clinic, a crèche, a day nursery, a dispensary, or a home or institution for the boarding, care and maintenance of children, old people, incapacitated persons or persons suffering from mental disability.

CLASS 14 – Use as an art gallery (not being a business premises), a museum, a public library or reading room, a public hall, an exhibition hall, a social centre, a community centre or a non-residential club, but not as a dance hall, music hall or concert hall.

CLASS 15 – Use as a theatre, a cinema, a music hall, a concert hall.

CLASS 16 – Use as a skating rink, or a gymnasium, or for indoor games or sports (including boxing, wrestling and bowling).

Sources

Butt, A., 1989. 'The impact of B1 on EC1'. *Estates Gazette*, 21 January 1989, pp.28–30.

Camping 1983. *Site Licensing of Camping Sites: Consultation Paper*. DOE, July 1983.

Circular No. 42 (1948). *Orders under Section 12(2)(f) and the Third Schedule*. Ministry of Town and Country Planning.

Circular No. 94 (1950). *The Town and Country Planning (Use Classes) Order. 1950*. Ministry of Town and Country Planning.

Circular 10/60. *Town and Country Planning General Development (Amendment) Order 1960; Town and Country Planning (Use Classes) (Amendment) Order 1960*. MHLG.

Circular 5/68. *The Use of Conditions in Planning Permissions*. MHLG.

Circular 1/85. *The Use of Conditions in Planning Permissions*. DOE.

Circular 14/85. *Development and Employment*. DOE.

Circular 13/87. *Change of Use of Buildings and Other Land: The Town and Country Planning (Use Classes) Order 1987*. DOE.

Command 9571 1985. *Lifting the Burden*. London, HMSO.

Command 9794 1986. *Building Businesses ... Not Barriers*. London, HMSO.

DCPN 1 1969. *General Principles*. Development control policy note. MHLG.

DCPN 8 1969. *Caravan sites*. Development control policy note. MHLG.

DCPN 9 1969. *Petrol Filling Stations and Motels*. Development control policy note. MHLG.

DCPN 11 1969. *Amusement Centres*. Development control policy note. MHLG.

DCPN 15 1975. *Hostels and Homes*. Development control policy note, DOE.

DC Statistics. *Development Control Statistics*. DOE, from 1974.

ET 1987. 'Councils fight to suppress mixed use development'. *Estate Times* Supplement, Autumn 1987.

Eve, J.R., 1987. *A Practical Guide to the 1987 Use Classes Order*.

Fay, C., and Rich, M. 1967. *Hill's Town and Country Planning Acts*. London, Butterworth.

GPM 1986. *Proposals to Modernise the Town and Country Planning (Use Classes) Order 1972*. DOE.

Grant, M., 1982. *Urban Planning Law*. London, Sweet & Maxwell.

Gwynedd, M., 1982. *Touring Caravans and Tents: Local Subject Plan*. Gwynedd County Council.

Hackney 1985. *Local Plan Consultation Draft*. London Borough of Hackney.

Hansard 1986. *Written Answers, Weekly Hansard, House of Lords,* vol. 476, No. 1330, cols. 719–20.

Home, R., Bloomfield, J., and Maclean, N., 1985. 'Trends in enforcement appeals'. *Estates Gazette,* vol. 276, 19 October 1985, pp.266–7.

Home, R.K., 1987a. 'Planning Decision Statistics and the Use Classes Debate'. *Journal of Planning and Environmental Law,* March 1987, pp. 167–73.

Home, R., 1987b. 'Trends in 'Planning Decision Statistics'. *Local Government Studies.*

Home, R., and Loew, S., 1987. *Covent Garden.* RICS Planning and Development Case Study No. 5. London, Surveyors Publications.

Humberside 1980. *Coastal Caravans and Camping Plan,* Humberside County Council.

Jackson, A., and Nabarro, R., 1986. *A Guide to Good Practice on Managed Workshop Schemes.* London, Investment Property Databank.

Jacobs, J., 1970. *The Economy of Cities.* London, Penguin.

James, D.E.H., 1973. *Notes on the Need for Planning Permission.* London, Oyez Publications.

James, N., and Pender, J., 1980. 'Solving the insoluble? Measures taken to tackle the summer influx of touring caravans and tents in West Cornwall'. *The Planner,* September 1980, pp.126–8.

King, W., 1987. 'The Future Roles in Town Centres'. *The Planner,* vol. 73, no. 4, April 1987, pp.18–22.

Kirby, D.A., and Holf, G.M., 1986. 'Planning responses to non-retail uses in shopping centres.' *The Planner,* vol. 72, no. 7, July 1986, pp.28–30.

Kirby, K., and Sopp, L., 1986. *Houses in Multiple Occupation in England and Wales.* Report of a Postal Survey of Local Authorities. HMSO, London.

Lamb, R., and Brand, J., 1983. 'Poor record shown on second wave.' *Planning Newspaper* 524, 24 June 1983, pp.8–9.

Mackenzie, R., 1988. 'Impact of the Use Class A on the High Street'. *Estates Gazette,* 1 October 1988, pp.20–21 & 96.

Markson, H.E. 1977. 'Use Classes Problems'. *Journal of Planning and Environmental Law,* pp.74–84.

Medway 1988. 'Medway Towns Local Plan Consultation Draft'. Rochester upon Medway City Council, Gillingham Borough Council, Maidstone Borough Council, Tonbridge & Malling Borough Council

Midgley, R., 1987. 'The Dwelling-House Use Class', *Journal of Planning and Environmental Law,* September 1987, pp.620–3.

Montgomery, J., 1986. 'The privatisation of public sector landholdings: the example of health authorities in London and the South East'. *Planning Practice and Research,* no. 1, September 1986, pp.23–6.

Norris, H., 1987. 'The New Use Classes Order', *Journal of Planning and Environmental Law,* December 1987, pp.819–36.

O'Sullivan, P., and Shepherd, K., 1984. *A Sourcebook on Planning Law in Ireland*. Professional Books Ltd, Abingdon.

Parmiter, J.C., 1988. 'The impact of B1', *Estates Gazette*, 14 May 1988, pp.119–20.

Planning Compensation 1986. *Compensation Provisions in the Town and Country Planning Acts*. Consultation paper, DOE.

PPG 1988. *Planning Policy Guidance Notes*. Department of the Environment.

Press Release 1987. 'Modernising planning controls over the use of property. No. 209, DOE, 6 May 1987.

Property Advisory Group (PAG) 1985. *Town and Country Planning (Use Classes) Order 1972: Report*. DOE.

RICS 1984a. *Amending the Use Classes Order to deal with high technology development*. Discussion paper, July 1984. GCPA/Report (84)28.

RICS 1984b. *Improvements and amendments to the planning system. Memorandum of observations*. GCPA/Report (84) 39.

RICS 1986a. *Town and Country Planning (Use Classes) Order 1972. Memorandum on the Property Advisory Group's report*. GCPA/Report (86) 3, February 1986.

RICS 1986b. *Proposals to modernise the Town and Country Planning (Use Classes) Order 1972. Memorandum of observations*. GCPA/Report (86)3, October 1986.

Robinson, S., and Purser, M., 1988. 'The B1 Shuffle'. *Estates Gazette*, 3 December 1988, pp.22, 23, 28.

RTPI 1986. *Proposals to modernise the Town and Country Planning (Use Classes) Order 1972. Memorandum of observations to the Department of the Environment on its consultation paper*. London, October 1986.

Smith, K., 1986. 'The HGV licensing system — under control at last?' *The Planner*, vol. 72, no. 4, April 1986, pp.21–2.

Titmuss Sainer and Webb 1987. *The 1987 Use Classes Order: does it achieve its aims?* Joint with Fuller Peiser. Available from 2 Serjeants' Inn, London EC4Y 1LT.

Walsh, P., Thomas, K., and Porter, J., 1986 *Home Based Economic Activity*, Oxford Polytechnic, Department of Town Planning, Working Paper No. 94.

Weatherill, P., 1988 *Land Use Gazetteer – The Comprehensive Guide to Land Uses and their Use Classes*. Leaf Coppin Publishing.

Westminster City Council 1983. *Quasi-industrial activities: non-statutory guidelines*.

Wilkinson, H.W., 1980. 'Planning law and undesirable activities.' *New Law Journal*, 20 November 1980, pp.1099–1101.

Table of Cases

Index